For Every Colle[
Begin Their Entrepreneurial Journey

THE IITM NEXUS

16 AMAZING JOURNEYS OF
IIT MADRAS GRADUATES
WHO TURNED INTO BUSINESS TYCOONS

SHREE PANDEY
DR SRIKANTH SUNDARARAJAN
SHIBANI SHASHIN

INDIA · SINGAPORE · MALAYSIA

Notion Press Media Pvt Ltd

No. 50, Chettiyar Agaram Main Road,
Vanagaram, Chennai, Tamil Nadu – 600 095

First Published by Notion Press 2022
Copyright © Shree Pandey, Dr Srikanth Sundararajan,
Shibani Shashin 2022
All Rights Reserved.

ISBN 978-1-68563-906-8

Contents

Keynote

This book is a testimony to the fruition of a vision that IIT Madras conceived and has nurtured over a decade and more. It is the vision to inspire, influence, and implant entrepreneurship integrally and organically within the Institute's ecosystem. Today, IIT Madras takes pride in its impeccable record of supporting the making of successful entrepreneurs, including illustrious alumni of IIT Madras who have made their Alma Mater stand tall with their brilliant achievements in the field of Entrepreneurship across the world.

The IIT ecosystem nurtures ideation, engages investment opportunities, and provides all it takes to convert innovative, out-of-the-box ideas into successful business ventures. The Institute hosts several initiatives and centers to promote excellence in innovation and entrepreneurship, besides forming sustained engagements with Industries, Academic Institutions across the world, Government bodies, and all associated stakeholders.

We are delighted to see our students, researchers, faculty, and alumni getting increasingly aware of the immense power and potential of translating cutting-edge research and innovation into products that will create an impact in the coming years. Many students and scholars today make an informed choice to forego jobs with lucrative salaries and explore entrepreneurship instead. It is encouraging to see this as it gives hope that the future of the country is vibrant in the hands of youngsters who dream big and are unafraid to pursue the difficult path to fulfill their dreams.

Almost all stories of Entrepreneurship are stories of dreams coming true. But almost never are they stories of dream journeys. They are stories of some advances but many more setbacks, of high successes and grounding failures, but there is rarely one of caving in to fear.

This book tells sixteen such success stories. More such stories are emerging in every nook and corner of the Institute every day. This book will be an inspiration for those with such stories in the making. May all such stories find their way to light. May this book be the first of many such volumes of success stories IIT Madras offers to the world.

– Bhaskar Ramamurthi, Director, IIT Madras

Introduction

By Prof. Ashok Jhunjhunwala
Faculty In-Charge IITM Research Park

The IITM Nexus is a collection of stories of 16 alumni entrepreneurs who appear to have nothing in common. Their graduation from IIT Madras spans from the mid-70s until the 2010s. They come from a large variety of backgrounds, some from the smaller towns of India, while others are from the Metros. Some come from vernacular backgrounds, while others are from the most modern schools of India.

Their academic performance at IITM is just as varied; some were institute toppers, while some just about did enough to graduate. They started their career in different ways and at different places and countries. Yet, going through their stories, one finds a common thread.

They all struggled before becoming successful entrepreneurs. They stumbled many times, even failed, yet never gave up. They struggled to support themselves through their journey. They often came across situations that would have led the ordinary to give up and settle for a job eventually. But they did not.

There was something in them that kept driving them. Of course, they succeeded and were lucky at times, but luck had deserted them many more times. It was hard work and long hours that finally worked in their favor. Equally important was their ability to form and work in a team.

These stories reinforce what is known about what makes entrepreneurs succeed today. Products and ideas play a minor role—preparation and planning, business plans, and market study help, but only up to a point. There are very few quick successes. Most take a long time and follow much toil and the ability to survive against all odds. Failure is okay, and so is being wrong. But one must learn from failures, continue to carry out deep analysis every time, and stay resilient. One must remember that each day is a new day.

IITM Start-up Ecosystem

While it may not be known, IITM has a long history of nurturing entrepreneurs. Somewhere in the mid-80s, we had learned that getting a large number of start-ups (the term "start-up" was not as ubiquitous then as it is today) may be the best way to develop India.

Some of us in the Electrical Engineering and Computer Science and Engineering department had started helping the start-ups. It started with one or two, but by the mid-90s, we had established this informal process. Youngsters with innovative ideas would work with faculty in projects and create products that would be commercialized.

IIT administration was a bit wary of this, and the overwhelming faculty opinion was that it would be wrong to bring in "Lakshmi" in a place where "Saraswathi" is worshiped. But this started changing at the turn of the century. There were talks about rules and regulations for faculty and student involvement in start-ups. By 2006, we formally set up a "Rural Technology and Business Incubator (RTBI)."

There was no looking back after the setting up of IITM Research Park. IITM Incubation cell (IITMIC) became the parent incubator and flourished along with RTBI, a Med Tech Incubator, a Biotech incubator, and an incubator called "Pravartak Technologies". It has incubated 245 companies so far and is considered India's most successful deep tech incubator.

The stories of start-up founders in this volume are a mix of those who grew as entrepreneurs before incubation activity started at IITM and those who were incubated at IITM. The stories demonstrate that IITM created a culture and laid the foundation for entrepreneurship from its early days.

Another common thing that we find in all the stories is that IIT's diverse experience, especially outside its classes, built personalities and flourished with time. I have personally known most of them; all I can say is that they were ordinary, and then they became extraordinary.

The Stories

Kedar Kulkarni learned and fulfilled his passion with Lema Labs, but succeeded big with Hyperverge, and that too, after his focus turned to the Indian market. Lema Labs have inspired a lot of youngsters to believe that technology is always within their grasp.

With international level chess players to Olympiad toppers as his classmates and their *Angreji Batein*, it would have indeed developed an inferiority complex within a small-town boy, *Sarvesh Agarwal*. IIT also provided him with enough confidence to create the most successful internship program through Internshala, which acts as a foundation stone today for tens of thousands of careers.

No one would have thought that the very ordinary *Satish Kannan* and his partner Enba, struggling at our lab with Solar-DC, would come up with a venture Medibuddy, which would go on to have a partner network of over 90,000 doctors, 7000 hospitals, 3000 diagnostic centers, and 2500 pharmacies.

Similar is the story of *Albin Jose*, who lived and had his make-shift office until recently in a perfectly ordinary and exceptionally mundane Bangalore flat, scattered with belongings, unwashed laundry, and unattended dishes in the sink. His LAL10 is the world's largest wholesale marketplace for sustainable products.

Gururaj Deshpande, one of the first highly successful entrepreneurs from IIT Madras, struggled and learned while making routers at Coral networks. He went on to have the most successful optical companies, Sycamore in the USA, and, more recently, Tejas Networks in India. But his passion today is the Deshpande Foundation, through which he would like to make an enormous impact on Indian society.

Kittu Kolluri ensured that his right brain was exercised significantly at IITM. As he learned the mantra of moving from Effective Leadership to Inspired leadership to Beloved Leadership, he later founded NEA and Neotribe Ventures to begin helping young ventures.

Anant Agarwal came from a small town to IITM, went to Stanford for his Ph.D., and became a renowned faculty at MIT. But he did not stop there; he came up with Harvard-MIT non-profit venture edX to make education a right for everyone, just like the air we breathe.

And then, there is a story of our own, *Satya Chakravarthy*, who returned to his alma mater to become a faculty. He created many breakthrough technologies, but his passion drove him to become a serial entrepreneur. His venture, Agnikul, is now the most promising space start-up in India. As the Co-founder and Technology lead of e-Plane, he would like to make a statement by designing hybrid-electric planes for short-range intercity travels that redefine urban mobility.

Anand Rajaraman recognized the need for a comparison shopping engine for classified listings on the web. Inspired by the song, "Yahoo! Chahe Koi Mujhe Junglee kahe," he named his venture "Junglee" to follow the then success of "Yahoo." The intellect of this

President's gold medalist at IITM helped him to justify this name, saying, "Internet is like this massive jungle of information, and people need someone (the Junglees) who knew their way around a jungle."

Tanmai Gopal's father was a faculty member at IITM, teaching German before he became an IAS officer. Tanmai joined IITM as a B. Tech student in the CSE department 25 years later. He was a potential gold medalist. But then, his focus was on product development and entrepreneurship. His latest venture Hasura provides developers with a GraphQL API to access their PostgreSQL, SQL, and MySQL databases. They have now open-sourced the product.

In his early career, **Amrit Acharya** worked with 200-300 suppliers and managed over 1000 workers at ITC. Today at Zetwerk, a marketplace for the manufacturing industry, he provides visibility on whether a supplier has received an order, started the manufacturing process, bought the raw material, finished the painting job, and whether the product is 70% ready or 90%. They have acquired around 250 odd customers and 2000 odd suppliers in India.

Before starting a start-up, *Rajiv Srivatsa* teaches us the value of multiple job experiences (Infosys, Yahoo). He built Urban-Ladder into a great company. But he also teaches us that when we think we have succeeded, things can fall apart. One needs to handle success and failure with humility and learn from both. The life of an entrepreneur is always a struggle.

Then, there are *Tarun and Daniel,* who founded Detect. This company has a simple product. It monitors large industrial operations of different kinds of process companies, whether oil and gas, chemical companies, power plants, or construction companies. Detect monitors the whole process continuously using various thermal, ultrasonics, and visual sensors (either fixed or mounted on a drone), get continuous data, monitor the process, and carry out analytics. What comes out is how to carry out operations better and provide warnings in advance when things go wrong. They are going places.

There is **Ram Krishna Verma.** Who would have thought this young boy from Rajasthan would one day build the most prominent company training youngsters for entrance exams at IITs? His perseverance paid off, and his "Resonance" is thorough; it takes kids to a different plane.

Sridhar Vembu is, of course, today's hero. When many dismissed Indian IT talent by parodying, "where is the product," this young man, who now prefers to operate from his native village in Thenkasi, uses raw IT talent of young Indians to build one of the largest IT product companies of our times. He believes that IITs are too elitist and international finance capital will never let India stand up. Having succeeded with ZOHO, he wants to build manufacturing in India in every sector so that the nation can stand tall.

The most vital part of the book, however, is the story of **Vineeta Singh.** She sought me out and sat next to me on a flight when she came to IITM. I knew then that this kid stranger is destined to go places and remember broaching the subject of entrepreneurship with her. I thought we had lost her to IIM. She did invite me to her marriage. But I had to leave early from Delhi. So, I was summoned to her bridal suite to bless her, where she was getting ready, and I gave her my blessings. I lost touch after that. But it came as no surprise that she founded and is driving Sugar Cosmetics today. Her story sums up the struggle that an entrepreneur has to go through.

Maybe we in India still have not learned to support our young entrepreneurs. But we are fast learning.

– Dr. Ashok Jhunjhunwala

Acknowledgment

It has been 35 plus years since I graduated from IIT Madras, and I still carry the learnings I gained from there. I felt this could be one of the ways to gather the learnings of Entrepreneurs and share it with the whole next generation of Indians.

Working with these remarkable entrepreneurs and chronicling their journey has indeed been exhilarating; add to this the extended team of students who made this possible, indeed a "for IITM, from IITM, and by IITM"— shining moment.

This work intends to instill entrepreneurship through inspiration, IITM being the backdrop purely because of convenience. The goal is to provide this impact far and wide beyond IITM.

Having had an interesting journey from 1984, spanning academia, corporate roles, being an entrepreneur, a professor, and an investor, I can relate to most events experienced by these brilliant entrepreneurs profiled here. In time, we will add more!

Finally, you can buy time, but it will not wait for you; you can own time, but it will disappear; befriend time, and it will teach you some invaluable lessons!

A very special thanks to all the Entrepreneurs and their teams, who gave their precious time to help build this book and constantly assist us.

I'm eternally grateful to Director Bhaskar Ramamurthy, Prof. Ashok Jhunjhunwala, and the whole IIT Madras administration for showering on us their mentorship.

A special thanks to the IITM Alumni association and all our alumni who came to help us at every point.

I want to thank our student friends who helped us regularly:

- Shruti Jain for going through every chapter multiple times and helping with the editing. Also, for managing Shree's firm so he can devote more time to the book.

- Nandhini Manwani for editing the book and helping us look at chapters from a layman perspective.

- Samruddhi Mokal for planning the marketing perspective of the book.

Writing a book isn't easy. The constant enthusiasm of my co-authors, Shree and Shibani, made sure that this book comes to reality and reaches all the students and young Entrepreneurs.

This project inspired me to keep pushing myself to get out of bed and the wheelchair because of an unfortunate stroke! Am really thankful to all who put their heart and soul into making this happen; there were many whose stories we could not cover because of their busy schedules; we intend to cover them soon in different forums!

Regards,

– **Srikanth Sundararajan**

Preface

Four years of college seems like a lifetime in itself for most of us. It's a whole different world where you enter as a naive youth and exit as an independent and capable individual. We might think that we will get all the clarity we need in this limited amount of time. But life is a wholly different ball game, and we often find that there is always more to the picture than meets the eye. This is our journey, where we discover what lies beyond that horizon.

In this book, we focused on the stories of some of our outstanding Alumni Entrepreneurs. We have explored their entire story, from childhood to getting into IIT and from there to finally making it big in life.

We ensured that we covered the stories of entrepreneurs from different decades and a plethora of different industries. This decision was deliberate so that each student has a role model whom they can look up to.

Our first important decision was to write the book in the first person. We wanted our readers to feel that the Entrepreneurs were directly talking to them in the environment of the Institute, just like seniors giving us Fundas.

Some stories go at a faster pace than others do. These people have been entrepreneurs for a very long time, and they have so much to share that an entire book's worth of words would not suffice.

A significant part of this book is written keeping IITM students in mind. Still, keeping our IITM values intact, we tried to democratize it as much as possible and have included references that can help everyone understand and enjoy the stories to the fullest.

It's tough to maintain uniformity while covering such a diversified spectrum of Industries (from Flying Cars to Cosmetics). We tried our best to ensure that there was not a lot of technical jargon. But there are a few places where the context is unclear without a basic understanding of that technology.

A crucial decision covered entrepreneurs from a range of decades, mainly for two reasons. One is to understand and appreciate the growth of India and IITs as an ecosystem for starting up, and to show the relentless efforts through the generations towards making it better. The second was to realize something that many of our classmates and we lack: patience, which Srikanth Sir emphasized. We had to show that sometimes, it can take decades to grow the empire and succeed.

Finally, Shiba and I, being students ourselves, have used this book several times as a guidance tool.

Have a great read, and feel free to mail us at shree.pandey99@gmail.com to share your views.

Warm Regards,

– **Shree and Shibani**

Introduction to Insti

○ Insti: Institute (Welcome to the insti slang)

○ IITM Research Park

The IIT Madras Research Park is a pioneering national effort to catalyze collaborative research between industry and academia, and enable technological innovation and nurture entrepreneurship. It houses the R&D and innovation wings of industry majors engaged in collaborative research and technology transfer with the faculty. The primary incubation cells under the IITMRP are:

○ Incubation Cell-IC

IITM IC seeks to nurture technology and knowledge-based ventures through their start-up phase by providing the necessary support to help entrepreneurs survive in the competitive market and reach a stage where they can scale up their ventures further.

○ Rural Technology and Business Incubator-RTBI

The RTBI uses business incubation as a strategy and methodology for rural and social development through capacity building, income generation, and services. It has since incubated over 30 companies. These ventures disseminate world-class technology to solve some of rural India's most challenging problems, such as power, water, and education.

○ E-Cell

E-Cell imbues the spirit of entrepreneurship in students and faculty community from various colleges across India, inspiring and encouraging them to take on entrepreneurial challenges and assisting them in launching and running business ventures. It has a plethora of yearlong events like Conclaves, Keynotes, Industry-defined Problems, B-Planning Competitions, and Workshops.

o   Centre for Innovation: CFI

Centre for Innovation (CFI) is the 'Student Lab' at IIT Madras. The industrious student innovators are connected, coached, and supported to nourish their skills and ideas to fully-fledged projects to compete in National and International Competitions.

o   Nirmaan

Nirmaan focuses on product development and encourages entrepreneurial ideas by providing seed funding for the start-ups led by students. It assists those with an idea at every step involved in converting it into a full-fledged incubated start-up.

o   GDC

The Gopalakrishnan Deshpande Centre for Innovation & Entrepreneurship (GDC) was established at IIT Madras in August 2017 to provide the necessary thought leadership and networking impetus to help build the systems and processes that enable innovative and entrepreneurial thinking across the Institute at all levels.

o   IITMAA

IITMAA represents about 45,000 plus IITM alumni in various chapters spread across the globe. The primary mission of IITMAA is to reconnect the alumni with their fellow alumni, institute, and students on the campus—engage through various activities among all the stakeholders—to generate Impact through several social and academic projects for collective growth.

o   Schroeter: Inter-hostel Sports Competition

o   LitSoc: Inter-hostel Cultural Competition

o   Tech Soc: Inter-hostel Tech related events

o   Shaastra

A student-run annual technical festival is the first such event in the world to be ISO 9001:2000 certified for implementing a Quality Management System. Shaastra is the annual technical festival of IIT Madras.

o   Saarang

Saarang is the annual, non-profit, and student-run cultural festival of IITM with the ISO certification of ISO 9001:2015 organization, making it the only one of its kind amongst college festivals.

o   Hostels

These are repetitively used in all the chapters so just for your info, Alakananda (Alak), Bhadra, Brahmaputra (Brahms), Cauvery, Ganga, Godavari (Godav), Jamuna (Jam), Krishna, Mahanadhi, Narmada, Pampa, Sabarmati, Saraswathi (Saras), Sarayu, Sharavathi (Sharav), Sindhu, Tamiraparani, Tapti, and Tunga.

Chapter 1

The Da Sugar Code

Vineeta Singh: Sugar Cosmetics

A tiny peek into early academic lives can remind us of that guy/girl who excelled in academics and aced sports too. But most of us will be filled with skepticism and disbelief if I told you about a visionary entrepreneur who is a record-breaking athlete as well. But that's the beauty of passion—it holds the strength to skyrocket human potential.

This is Vineeta's story—a story bound to shatter some glass ceilings and break many stereotypes.

A Delhi-ite restyled in Madras

In 2001, writing the Joint Entrance Exam with lakhs of other IIT aspirants, I too had my notions about how IITs ought to be, '*I shall be a mechanical engineer and finally experience the thrill of living in a hostel.*' With my results, I could get Mechanical Engineering at IIT Delhi. What a jackpot, right? But as it turns out, there was something else bothering me.

Even though IIT Delhi was a top choice, it was just a couple of kilometers away from home, implying that I would miss hostel life, which was an important part of my college aspirations. Growing up in Delhi comes with many restrictions for young women, and I wanted to break free from those by living independently in a hostel in a different city. So, the next best option seemed like Electrical Engineering at IIT Madras. Chasing a more sought-after branch than the one I was getting at IIT Delhi was probably the only way to convince my parents about my decision. Madras was as far away from Delhi as possible—literally on the opposite side of the country! But my parents, who have been academics in their own profession, agreed to my line of argument, and that's the story of how I came to be here!

Life at IIT Madras

But suddenly, I faced a very different predicament now. Having given up the branch I always dreamt of pursuing, I learned much later about how "dreaded" the Electrical Engineering department of IIT Madras was. To add to that, I was in for more change than I had expected after shifting from Delhi to Chennai. Chennai was not very cosmopolitan back in 2001. There was the obvious cultural difference experienced by a North Indian who moved to Chennai for the first time. The food at the hostel didn't agree with my palate as I'd grown up being quite fond of my mother's home-cooked meals. And to top things off, the skewed gender ratio typical of IITs (24/440 in our batch) placed me in a very different dynamic from my earlier academic cohorts.

During my campus life, I took a couple of organizational roles that included being a Core Group Member at Shaastra and Sports Secretary at Sharavati Hostel. Being a part of the Inter-IIT team for all four years, I also developed a close connection with sports, which continued even after IIT Madras and played a significant role in my life. By the end of the second year, I realized electrical engineering was something I wouldn't be able to do for the rest of my life. This, combined with the fact that I enjoyed organizational roles, led me to explore my industrial inclination, and an internship was the best way to do so.

Fortunately, I was able to grab a coveted internship at ITC and subsequently earned a PPO (Pre-Placement Offer). While most students were applying for an MS or Ph.D. in America, I decided to take the CAT and got through IIM Ahmedabad.

Today, when I look back at the time I spent at IIT Madras, I am acutely aware of my tendency to avoid risks. The initial disconnect I faced after joining IIT Madras, and my average academic performance at the institute made me think that this was the outcome of me going against the rules for the first time in my life. So, I decided that I had taken enough risks and should play safe now.

Even in the middle of all this, my inter-IIT coach urged me to participate in athletics and basketball as my height would be advantageous. But I was so afraid of an injury and losing my gold in Badminton that I never tried any other sport. While graduating, I had a chance at the "Insti blues" and didn't even apply as I did not want to risk the embarrassment of losing. During my internship at ITC, the production manager's assistant told me that my dressing, which was regular jeans and tops, was attracting a lot of attention in the factory. Extremely tense, I called my mother from Delhi to Saharanpur to bring me baggy jeans and oversized men's shirts so that my clothes wouldn't put my PPO at risk.

Such was my fear of failing during my IIT days.

Introduction to Entrepreneurship

On my first flight to Madras from Delhi, I was busy imagining what college would be like when I overheard someone say that he is a professor from IIT Madras. I got excited and swapped my seat to sit close to the professor. When he offered his visiting card, it read "Professor Jhunjhunwala, Head of Department, Electrical Engineering," and I froze as I'd been told that he was one of the most dreaded professors of the most dreaded department across IITs. He started the conversation by grilling me on a spectrum of things ranging from theoretical questions like the difference between analog and digital signal to questions like, "Why aren't there more women in engineering?"

Professor Jhunjhunwala gets to you while he speaks, and so bit by bit, the conversation took shape and ended up pivotal in my goals and aspirations.

He asked me, "What do you want out of life?"

I answered the question honestly and said I would be happy when I was rich and could travel the world independently.

To this, he gave an experienced laugh and said, "I have seen enough people in my life to assure you that getting rich doesn't make you happy. From what you've shared so far, I think you should consider becoming an entrepreneur. Seems like something you'd enjoy."

I didn't think much about it then, but the concept of entrepreneurship being fun had just been seeded in my head.

A few years later, when I started exploring the question, "If not engineering, then what next?" it was entrepreneurship that I first started reading about. The biographies of Steve Jobs, Richard Branson, and Howard Schultz were some of the books I read back then. Further, I loved my internship at ITC. I loved the whole feel of working in a factory, making minor improvements, and measuring their impact in the larger scheme of things. So, the inspiration from all the books I read, loving the organizational activities I did on campus, and thoroughly enjoying my internship at ITC gave me a clear vision at the end of four years that I would run my own business someday.

So, when I had calls from all the IIMs. in my fourth year, I decided to go to IIM Ahmedabad because of a course on entrepreneurship called LEM (Leadership and Entrepreneurial Motivation) that was taught there. I was so convinced of this decision that I told my parents while taking the CAT that if IIM Ahmedabad didn't work out, I'd work for a year and try my luck again because LEM was going to be the most important course of my business school education.

Paradoxically, the year I joined IIM Ahmedabad, LEM got canceled as Professor Sunil Handa, who taught the course, was unwell and decided to skip one batch.

I showed up at his house and begged him to reconsider, "Sir, you can't cancel this course. It defeats my entire purpose of coming to study here."

So, finally, to get rid of the crazy student at his doorstep, he agreed to do a two to three-day workshop for our batch!

Start-up ka Keeda (The Start-up Bug)

Even though I had it clear in my mind that I had to be an entrepreneur someday, "when" was always the biggest question. But many things panned out at IIM Ahmedabad, such that I decided just after college was the best time.

Firstly, I took a few moonshots like contesting the elections on campus, applying for the Best Woman All Rounder award, and signing up for a marathon. While everything wouldn't go in my favor, I started enjoying taking risks, even if that came with some failures! When you are terrified of failing, and you see yourself get past some of those fears, it's exhilarating. I found myself getting addicted to that feeling. It seemed like a cue for the entrepreneur in me to finally unleash herself.

Secondly, my conversations with Professor Handa validated my desire to start right after college. He made me realize that since I didn't know what living like an investment banker meant (I had received a Pre-Placement Offer from Deutsche bank), it would be easier to give that up now than after getting used to a big paycheck every month. Thirdly, I was lucky to have the company of three batchmates, who were equally passionate about starting up. So, it seemed like a brilliant idea for us to start this company together.

Onward

The first idea we stumbled upon was to start a lingerie brand. My internship at Deutsche Bank required me to visit London and New York for a month each. I observed an entirely different level of product quality and variety available to women in both places. India stood nowhere close to that standard. Even the shopping experience was fabulous compared to the over-the-counter "hosiery" shops that most Indian women shopped at. We interviewed many women and realized a massive opportunity and market for creating a lingerie brand in the country and started to shoot straight at it.

Then came the first of many twists and hurdles I was about to face in the years to come. Since we needed to raise capital for production and our go-to-market strategy, we tried fundraising. But the VCs paid no heed to us as we were fresh out of college and consumer brands weren't very "fundable" back then. Disappointed but not ready to quit, we jumped on the next best option, a bootstrapped human resources outsourcing company, Quetzal. Since these services were commoditized and customers were price sensitive, there wasn't much scope for innovation, but we soldiered on. We tried to scale the business for five years, but it didn't go too far, and internal differences of opinion forced us to part ways.

This incident felt like my biggest failure at that time. While I was at the peak of self-doubt, I started realizing that this was probably a sign that I should build a company in a space that I'm more passionate about. That brought me back to women consumers and figuring out how to bring international quality products to India. With a small sum of seed capital that I could get at the time of my exit from Quetzal, I decided to launch a beauty products subscription company for women. My husband, Kaushik, who was working at McKinsey then, built the e-commerce store for the company, and we realized we had complementary skills. So, once the business started getting initial traction, he decided to come on board full time.

By 2013, we had raised our seed round to scale the e-commerce business, and in the process, started seeing the glaring white space in the cosmetics category. While we were able to reach young millennial women via social media and started gaining online traction to shop only, we couldn't meet their desire for international quality makeup products that suited Indian skin tones and climatic conditions. The other thing we quickly realized was that most large brands were too busy fighting shelf space battles with retailers to notice how fast the consumer's tastes were evolving.

Eventually, armed with compelling insights on what millennial women wanted from beauty brands, we decided to launch SUGAR as a cosmetics brand that created textures and shades that were perfect for young India. While we didn't have much capital left, and the beauty subscription business wasn't too profitable, we cut down all costs and took a small loan from a couple of friends and my mom.

We launched with two products: the first matte eyeliner in India and a water-proof kajal. As we'd spent three years sharpening our consumer insight and then researching products, both launches had fantastic feedback, and customers loved them. More than 1000 customers came back with five-star reviews. People started asking why it wasn't available on other e-Commerce shopping portals like Nykaa, Amazon, etc. Soon, we started talking to e-commerce websites for listing the brand. While they loved the products, we wouldn't be considered a legitimate brand without at least a few more lipsticks in our range. While we had formulated and manufactured four shades of lipsticks that we knew would be superhits, unfortunately, we ran out of money to import them.

With no solution in sight, we went back to our first angel investor, India Quotient, and explained to them our dire situation. While they could not officially invest any more funds in the company as the traction wasn't enough with two products to merit a proper follow-on round, they could see our conviction and had faith in our resilience. Something magical happened then! The partners at the fund agreed to give us one crore from their own fund fees at a nominal interest rate with an earnest disclaimer that if this went down, they would be in trouble.

So, we just HAD to make this work. And we made that last one crore of capital really count. We launched crayon lipsticks, made them available on Nykaa and Amazon. As more and more customers started discovering SUGAR, the brand grew virally. We built a complete makeup range, grew distribution to 10,000 outlets, and continue to be one of the most social media savvy brands, loved by millennial and gen-z women. The product-market fit was great. So, subsequent fundraising was easier, and SUGAR is now ranked amongst India's top five makeup brands.

Everything Sports

I have had a lifelong association with sports and more so after graduation. Kaushik and I also became the first couple in India to complete the IRONMAN triathlon, widely regarded as the most challenging single-day endurance event. It entails a 3.8 km swim + 180 km bike + 42.2 km run to be completed in under 17 hours.

I love endurance races because it's like a zip version of entrepreneurship. Moving past your fears, looking stupid to the outside world, and keeping the faith that you will make it happen— the whole roller coaster ride in a span of six months (as opposed to ten years that a typical business takes to scale). One day, you have a big win or reach a significant milestone, and the next day, suddenly, there's a setback. These passions of mine require a ton of madness, patience, and resilience.

Initially, as I signed up for the Ironman within a year of delivering a baby and without knowing how to swim 100 meters or ever having ridden a road bike, it seemed like the craziest idea! So, there was this whole period of self-doubt, failing, having awful days, and somehow, finding the strength to battle through it all, showing up at the start line, and then completing the race within cutoff.

(Vineeta completed the 89 km Comrades Ultramarathon thrice between 2012 and 2014. She also earned podium finishes at the Delhi International Triathlon 2017, the Hyderabad Triathlon 2016, the Chennai 3/4th Iron Triathlon 2016, and the Nashik Half Marathon 2013. She also ran a half marathon in the 6th month of pregnancy back in 2018 to build advocacy on a healthy pregnancy.)

What difference did being a woman make?

When I joined IIT Madras, I thought being on the minority side was my advantage, as whenever I made a point, it would be heard as I had a unique voice. But over the years, I started to see the flip side of things. I realized there aren't many women anywhere I go, from engineering to B-School to fundraising. This means there aren't enough role models, mentors, or cheerleaders. There are some challenges that only women face, and it's always inspiring to have more representation.

Another common trend in industries where women are in the minority is to reduce their achievements to their gender rather than their capability. When I got a PPO at Deutsche Bank during my internship at IIM Ahmedabad, it was quite coveted. It was the first time an investment bank offered an Associate role at an Indian business school. But the narrative would often turn to this being on account of an unsaid diversity quota. The same justification would apply to all my accomplishments at IIT. Once, while fundraising, I was explicitly told that the odds would be low without a male co-founder. So, I do feel that women have to keep proving their worth repeatedly until they learn how to turn a deaf ear to all the questioning and judgment.

My goal is to build a company that does not link capability to gender and has many, many role models for both women and men. We employ 1400+ women at SUGAR, and I keep reminding them to be whomever they want to be every single day without worrying about the labels and limits imposed by others. As I have learned through my journey, once we are okay to move past failures and rejections, there is not much that can really stop us from making the journey to where we want to be.

Chapter 2

The Zorro from Zoho

Sridhar Vembu: ZOHO Corporation

Running a 1.83 billion-dollar company from a rural village in Tamil Nadu is no mean feat. But the founder and CEO of ZOHO Corporation (an Indian multinational technology company), Sridhar Vembu, makes it seem effortless as he strolls through the village roads in his homely sandals, adorned in a shirt and Mundu. Imagine a billionaire whose daily routine includes cycling around a rural neighborhood and looking after the vegetables in his garden.

As unprecedented as it sounds, Vembu believes that his rural endeavor could pave the way for sustainable workforce generation in the current scenarios of an increasingly urban-driven industry. (More on this ahead.) Mr. Vembu hosts considerable disdain towards the word "conventional". Out of the gazillion things that an entrepreneur could learn from him, the most vital would be his resolve and faith in his decisions. He turned down VC funds for Zoho and has never looked back since. In the age when starting up means chasing after venture capital funding and IPOs, ZOHO Corporation has been operating privately for over 20 years, with Sridhar owning 88% of its shares. Mr. Vembu, alternatively called the "bootstrap king", has established Zoho as one of the most formidable software companies in the world.

Despite having a prestigious educational background himself, Vembu is quite averse to the idea of elitist educational institutions. He aims to correct this disparity with his initiative—ZOHO University. Here is a place where 'contextual learning', as Vembu likes to call it, is at the core of all activities. Vembu staunchly believes that grades never correlate with professional success. With the proper training and commitment, you can generate a robust workforce with any student base irrespective of their college or degree. Today, 10% of the workforce in Zoho is a product of Zoho University, and many more young individuals continue to benefit from this exceptional endeavor.

Vembu does not compromise with principles. Some even call him arrogant, but belief is not a matter of choice but conviction. And he lives by that saying. Let's step into his shoes for a while and embark on his tumultuous journey through entrepreneurship.

Never a follower

An obvious choice for an AIR 27 in JEE would be Computer Science at IIT, even back in 1985. But I chose the Electrical Engineering branch because the notions that I had about CSE at that time did not agree with me. I believed that I would have more hands-on experience in education with EE.

IITM was close to home. But when I came to campus, it was a cultural shock for me. However, I would argue that I was more of a surprise to my batchmates than they were to me. Most of the kids were from very high-end English medium schools, and I was from a Tamil Medium school. They used to play their whacky English tunes on speakers and were bewildered to know that I had not heard nor had any intention to listen to these so-called "trendy songs". I knew what I liked and what I did not and never gave in to trends.

Should IITs Even Exist?

The question "Why?" has been fundamental to me throughout my life. Studying in an elite government institution that provided me with a top-notch education forced me to wonder, "Should IITs even exist?"

The answer leaned towards the negative because I did not feel that we were giving back much to the nation as IITians. But that is just one side of the equation. All through college, I only came across what I have come to identify as "context-free education". You spend a lot of time gathering knowledge, but ultimately, you do not know what to do with it (hence, the term context-free). In the end, you get a degree from IIT, but I think that four dedicated years of your life is a steep price to pay. All in all, it seems like a lose-lose situation.

This was the first article I ever wrote, and it got published in the institute magazine, *Focus*. The director called me to his office. Because, obviously, it was not a good thing for me to say. But everyone knew that I was saying something that needed to be told, and I don't regret any of it. If anything, this view of the education system has only reinforced itself in my mind after all these years as a student and, recently, as a teacher at ZOHO University.

Princeton

After IITM, I went abroad to complete my Ph.D. at Princeton before being offered a job as a lecturer at Australian National University in Canberra. While I did take the job then, I realized this ebbing within me that my heart was not in this. It did not feel right. I apologized to them and said I could not carry on this job in all good conscience. Technically, I am a post-doctorate, but I never assumed the title. I didn't believe in the work I did there. So, I hung up all my academic ambitions.

Qualcomm

I decided to start from scratch. I was an Electrical Engineer with a newfound interest in software development, which I had recently been introduced to. I took a job in Qualcomm in 1994 in San Diego. I worked in wireless communications, including CDMA and Power Control, for about two years as an electrical engineer. The mathematical challenges there appealed to me, and I finally found a context in my learning. I realized I really did like this kind of work. But alas! I left that place because I really wanted to do something of my own in India. I wanted to contribute to a more significant cause. My long ebbing thirst for the independent endeavor was finally about to be quenched.

The Advent of ZOHO

Driven by the prospect of starting up a software company in India, I started "**AdventNet**" along with two of my brothers, Sekar and Kumar, and Tony Thomas, in 1996 from a small apartment in the suburbs of Chennai.

Initially, we worked with network management. We were making enough money to survive. Originally, Tony served as the CEO and Chairman of the company, with me working as its Chief Advertiser. I began to interact with customers in the Bay Area, focusing on improving and selling the technology the company sold.

Initially, we were deep into **SNMP (Simple Network Management Protocol)**. Niche markets are the best targets for bootstrappers. You automatically get a steady consumer base. But with niche markets, you can only grow so much. How you pivot from there is crucial. We evolved by offering installable products for Enterprise and IT Management under our Manage Engine brand.

Having spent some time in sales, I had learned how to get consumers on board. Getting a sale is like getting a date; you have to be shameless. The cross-product adoption amongst our existing customers really helped us sustain our product even though we were outspent by our competitors 1:20 with respect to marketing.

Patience v/s Pride

In 2000, which also happens to be when we expanded official operations in Japan, I got a term sheet from a VC firm with all their clauses listed. I had no intention to exit the company at any point, and that did not agree with their exit clauses. What would I do after an exit? That is an excellent question to ask yourself before you take on funding.

I was told that this is a standard VC clause. I told them that I was not a standard entrepreneur then. So be it. I never was one to follow through with trends. I was not about to give in this time when I was finally doing work that I cared about. Funding, to me, was not necessarily a celebratory event. There are a lot of strings attached, and the pressure to deliver is immense. Patience is vital in entrepreneurship, and there are numerous unknowns. I believed that if we could survive, we would find a way to thrive.

A conventional start-up may overlook that a vast majority of acquisitions fail, and it's the customer that pays the price. Many of our products were developed to meet our own needs— for Zoho itself runs entirely on Zoho. This means our software often must fail us before it can fail you.

We would reinvest in ourselves from our profits and become our own VCs. Most of our profits go towards R&D and making the product better for the consumer. We do not need to be told what good business looks like. It's never about how much money you have in your account. It's about the exciting things you can do with it. We are private but far from small, with nearly 7,000 employees across the globe. Our style of unconventional thinking seems to have paid off.

Riding the market waves

Eventually, we evolved from products to SaaS (Software as a Service), but the cost of consumer acquisition in that field had skyrocketed. Keywords on web browsers are costly. We do not even spend half as much as our competitors spend on marketing. Our best bet was to cross-promote products to customers we had already acquired. We pivoted towards CRM in 2005 with Zoho CRM, which helps salespeople reach more prospects, engage them in real-time and close deals faster.

By 2008, we had Projects, Creator, Show, Sheet, Zoho Docs, and Zoho Meeting. This cloud-based software was up and running and clocked 1 million users by August of that year. We owe it to our customers. With them, we have continued to stay private and profitable.

ZOHO Corporation

In 2009, we renamed the company to ZOHO corporation. By then, we provided a whole set of services that came under our umbrella. Zoho Corporation became the umbrella company of three different divisions that cater to three other markets.

ZOHO was named after an online office suite service that the company provided at the time (quite like the Microsoft Office suite).

A success story

Whatever profits we made, a significant part of it went into R&D, which created more revenue for us. We never felt the need to raise funding, partly because we were patient and partly because we believed in the quality of our product. The engineering behind them was robust, and we knew how to sell to our customers. Over the years, we have made our services so comprehensive and versatile that even a catastrophic failure in one of the markets would not leave us bleeding. Diversification is what has kept us kicking in the face of our competitors. We are always coming up with new products. And they have always paid off for us.

Remember, always focus on the next relevant step. Anything worth doing takes a lot of patience. You may get lucky, but you can't wait for that to happen. You should be aware of your means to pursue a market based on its transience. Entrepreneurship is not about making quick bucks. You have to be in it for the long haul if you want to make a difference.

In 2015, we reached a 15 million user landmark, a significant achievement for us at that time. We knew we were doing something right. 2015 was a hectic year for us: We launched six applications across sales, marketing, communication, and finance.

ZOHO Schools and ZU

We fell upon a very crucial realization through my brother, Mani. He did not have a perfect educational background. Kumar was operating in India back then, and he brought on Mani to work with him. And within a few months of training, we saw surprisingly great results with him. We could draw parallels with similar experiences, and we realized that grades/ credentials and work skills do not correlate well.

We came up with this initiative to train our own workforce straight out of high schools. And we could offer them something mainstream colleges could not—jobs right after completing their programs. Our values, too, were very different from that of mainstream colleges. We focused on contextual education. And we made sure to give everyone a chance to excel regardless of their former educational background.

Our process is simple—we select high school students from government schools in Chennai and surrounding cities. These students then pursue 18-month internships in mathematics, computer science, and English, including six-month training within the organization. The syllabus is constantly revised to ensure that the syllabus is up to date with the latest technological developments. They are given a monthly stipend during the training period. Nothing can prepare you for the industry like tackling the practical challenges of working as a developer.

We focus a lot on peer-to-peer learning and encourage self-initiated projects. The significant upside to practical and hands-on learning is that it boosts your confidence, and you get immediate feedback for your work. It also initiates you to real-time problem-solving, which thus, reinforces your concepts.

We aim to eliminate prestige as a factor that dictates the quality of your education. All you need to learn are curiosity and zeal. If you want to work hard for a goal, put that effort into contextual education rather than test-taking skills. As students, we should all be curious about alternative models of learning.

The success of Zoho schools will be when they do not need to exist. Education in India really needs a revamp, and we all need to get out of this prestige trap. It's regressive, and it hinders any real growth. Our end is effective and sustainable workforce generation. We are learning to produce what we consume. Above grades and gratification, we need to upgrade our skills, dive more profoundly, and enjoy the fruits of real learning.

A CEO's Guide to Gardening

We take in students from rural backgrounds straight out of high school, and we give them the necessary tools, and a means to develop their skill set. Most of them end up getting jobs at Zoho itself, but of course, they are free to aim higher and take their journey forward. But many of them prefer to stay back home, away from the crowds of the cities. Many migrants are reluctant to leave their hometowns, but they feel compelled due to their limited means. Here, we provide them with the best employment opportunities near their homes! Zoho schools power about 15% of the Zoho workforce. We have built a resilient web of peer-to-peer learning, where students can get industry experience as they learn. That is also one of the benefits of going rural.

We are currently experimenting with ten villages in Tamil Nadu, where 200 of its engineers— 20 in each town—will collaborate and build software for the world. These feeder offices are situated 20-30 kilometers away from their hometowns.

Migration to cities searching for better means of livelihood removes the villages of their intellectual topsoil. Suppose you devoid a land of its topsoil, it becomes infertile (which is the condition of the small towns and villages due to mass migration). An excess of topsoil concentration also makes the soil infertile (which is what happens to cities with an influx of migrants). Distribute the topsoil evenly, and you have fertile land that will yield a healthy crop! Initially, we grew very fast in a transient market. But what now?

You always need to tap into a durable trend to be a stable business. Going rural might be a trend worth tapping into. I believe it to be pivotal in the journey towards Atma Nirbhar Bhaarat. The rural population is like a garden replete with fresh produce just waiting to be plucked.

Finances—A philosophy

All business questions boil down to economics. That's why I am always up to date about what transpires in the industry. 90% of our revenues are clocked outside India. I need to stay ahead of the curve to adapt to market trends. The way the world is run doesn't foster confidence for the top-level decision-makers. I have and always will believe in independent thinking.

Our business strategy is all about symmetry and resilience. In this transient world, you just CANNOT afford to rely on just one thing even if it makes you rich! Hyper specialization does not work. Because wealth implies resilience, it means the ability to withstand adversity and self-reliance.

Why me?

"Man does not live for bread alone." Money cannot keep your people with you. It's about fairness. It's about keeping honest expectations and meeting them. As a leader, it is an excellent question to ask yourself, "**Why should people work for me?**" Leadership questions have to be very much personal. Because it is you who will be accountable at the end of it all. For people, I believe the sooner you learn responsibility, the better. That is why I encourage the idea that students should start earning from the age of 20. The best education is character building.

"Life is a box of chocolates. You never know what you're going to get."

Chapter 3

Rags to Resonance

R K Verma: Resonance Eduventures

Mr. Ram Kishan Verma was born in a small village in the Kota district of Rajasthan. Academic excellence was synonymous with him throughout his life. He instilled the same zeal for learning in his students during his many years of teaching. He became very popular among the student fraternity, as RKV Sir, for his in-depth subject knowledge, unmatched teaching skills, and passionate aptitude for the coaching profession.

The dream of becoming an edupreneur resulted in the genesis of Resonance, founded by Mr. R. K. Verma in 2001 at Kota. Since then, Resonance has taken several leaps and bounds forward under his leadership and persistent quest to take it to the pinnacle of success and excellence.

Humble Origins

I hail from a remote village in the Kota district. My father was a stone miner in Khan Kumbkot, which houses the famous Kota stone quarries. It's somewhat ironic that I came to work for an industry that made Kota famous.

Although I did not have a very fancy education like kids in bigger cities, the teachers at the government school I was studying in recognized that I was a bright student. Despite his limited means, I am grateful that my father made sure that I completed my schooling.

I always had a flair for mathematics. But I was so underexposed to the fast-paced, mainstream education system that I never knew about Physics, Chemistry, and such until the 9th grade.

From grades 9th to 12th, I studied in a school in Ramganj Mandi, which was 10 km away from my village. I fondly remember I used to span that distance on a cycle every single day. But it was never a burden for me. I was so excited at the prospect of learning that I did not mind the grind at all. My parents were not well educated in school, but I learned a lot of important lessons from them. One of them was resilience. I was not afraid to work hard for what I wanted and accepted every challenge life threw at me.

JEE preparations

I was always bright in studies during school, but the things that were a great challenge to me at that time were:

1. Lack of exposure

2. The language gap

I talked to a distant relative of mine who studied at a polytechnic college in Kota, and he once visited our home when I was in the 10th grade. He was the one who introduced me to JEE. He recognized my zeal to learn and said I should go for JEE to make it. We had a discussion, and I asked him more about the profession. He developed an image of IITs for me, traveling on flights and living a very successful life. Although my initial notions were a bit naive, I knew then that this was what I wanted to do.

I could not afford tuition/coaching at the time (How ironic). So, I bought a bunch of JEE preparation books from a book shop in Kota and just dove right in. They were all in English, which posed another challenge. But I caught up fast and could soon understand the language well enough to solve problems.

The IITM Journey

I was exposed to an entirely new atmosphere the *minute* I stepped foot at Madras Railway Station. The language was different; the people were different. It was a cultural shock for me. I had always been introverted as a kid, and my lack of exposure reinforced that. I was apprehensive about adjusting to this very unfamiliar territory. It was also the first time that I would be away from my parents for such a long period of time. Madras is a long way from Kota.

But I had a goal in mind. I wanted to become something. I had to spend four years in this institution and learn. So, with a heavy heart, I bid adieu to Pitaji (my father) and began my journey at IITM.

Being from a Hindi medium school, I felt like a black sheep amongst hundreds of my peers who could speak English and shoot out words like a machine gun. Being an introvert did not help my situation much. It's not like I did not have friends at all, but I could not resonate with people a lot. The teaching mode of professors was also English, and it took me some time to catch up with what was being taught in class. But I was catching on.

I don't claim that my transformation at IITM bore any resemblance to the rebirth of a phoenix or the metamorphosis of a butterfly. It was gradual but definite. I slowly started doing things outside my comfort zone and building up my confidence together piece by piece. I did not take up any major responsibilities during my time in college, as I was still trying to fit in somehow. But eventually, I did fit in, and IIT helped me build the foundation of the confidence that would fuel all my future endeavors.

At the end of the first year of my B.Tech. program, I got my passport card made. It was a common practice for B.Tech graduates to go abroad for further studies. I wrote about it in my letter to Mummyji, my mother (letters were a thing back then). She did not know what a passport was; the only card we had back at the village was a ration card, which we used to procure sugar, kerosene, rice, grains, etc., at concessional rates.

I explained to her that one uses this if one has to go to foreign lands outside India. My mother was a simple-minded but strong lady. She never went to school or learned to write. So, she made the neighbor write a letter for her.

She told me, "You are so far away from the village that it already seems like you are in a foreign land to us. We sent you far away to study and become somebody to take care of the people back home/village and do something for them. No one in our village has reached as far as you have. You have a duty to this place."

My parents' words have always been a guiding light for me throughout my life. So, I decided not to go abroad and stay and do something for my village/country.

Civil Services – An endeavor

At the time, entrepreneurship was just a word we used to hear thrown around in talks and seminars. But I never really got an idea of what it meant. I wanted to get into Civil services based on what people said back home. So, I decided to appear for the IAS exam.

I did sit for campus interviews at the time and accepted the offer from BHEL Jhansi under the assumption that I would get enough time to prepare for my exam, given that it's a government sector job. I cleared pre in the first attempt by taking Physics.

Let me backtrack a little and address the situation back home. My father used to work in a mine as a day laborer. That is how he supported all of us. I asked for his advice on what I should do next. I was about to go for the final exam for IAS and needed time to prepare. I could play it safe and juggle my job along with the preparations, or I could resign and give my all to the preparations. My father had backed me through all my educational endeavors. I felt a powerful urge to take the safer option for the sake of my family.

But what my father said brought me to tears. He said, "Don't worry, son. *Mein tujhe aur dass saal tak padhaa sakta hu.* (I can support your education for another 10 years if I have to). Leave your job and work hard for your exams. No one will be happier than me if you succeed."

Hearing this was like an energy boost for me. The fact that my dad was ready to risk the stability of my well-paying job for my dreams made me believe in them even more. I started my preparation for the exam in full swing. I bought old study material from Brilliant Tutorials.

After I appeared for the mains exam in Jaipur, I searched for a job while I waited for the results (I was hopeful that it would pay out for me). I figured that I could use my degree and land a coaching job. I applied to a lot of coaching places but could not find work as I was very inexperienced. I was lacking in my presentation and speaking skills.

Then one day, a friend of mine from my school days set me up as a tutor to the son of the school principal in Jaipur. And when I came to my village for a day, my school teachers permitted me to take tuitions for their students. Eventually, word spread by word of mouth, and I got into tutoring in Physics, Maths, Science, and English about 10 students of grades 3rd–12th at their homes in Ramganj Mandi. Even those who used to go to Ramganj Mandi from my village for 11th and 12th PCMB schooling started coming to learn from me at my house in the evening/night. I taught these students for free.

At the time, my prime objective in teaching was to stay in touch with my studies in case I had to reappear for the IAS exam. But a stronger, somewhat more primal motive was to keep up my social skills, especially to remove my fear of speaking in front of others. I knew that I had to go out there and face my fear of public encounters, something I would have to deal with a lot if I were to become an IAS officer. Also, I could contribute at home to make both ends meet.

Now, if this were a Hindi Movie, I would be delighted to tell you that I cleared that exam. But that did not happen. I was pretty disheartened. It was the first time my exam results had not come through successfully. But later, I read the interviews of the rankers in the exam who had cleared the paper in their second attempt, some even in their fifth one! That gave me the confidence to try again.

Initiation to the coaching scenario

In the aftermath, I applied to Bansal Classes and was selected. Bansal Sir used to teach Maths to all students and Physics to class 11th people. I was given the responsibility to teach Physics. Bansal Sir hired me because of my honesty, self-motivation, hard work, humbleness, passion, and how I studied independently because my presentation skills were not up to the mark then.

Admittedly, I initially could not stand up to his teaching standards, as I was just at par with my social skills. But I started working very hard to improve my teaching methods. There were a lot of English medium students who were not very satisfied with my teaching. So, I used to wait after class and take extra classes. I even called them home to study/clear doubts personally. So, in a way, I made up for my inferiority complex with more genuine and thoughtful interaction to bridge the gaps in my teaching. The students from weak backgrounds were able to connect a lot with me. I was doing everything needed, from running day-to-day errands like making and collecting papers and checking or distributing sheets to taking classes at odd times when no one wanted to.

I was so immersed in improving my teaching and challenging my limits every day at the coaching centre that I left the goal of becoming an IAS officer way behind. Teaching these students and coming up with new ways to tackle the learning curve became my first nature. I worked day and night to be able to deliver the perfect lecture. Bansal Sir was already a very accomplished teacher, and I realized I had to up my game to reach his level.

I always looked after my studies. I had little help from any coaching throughout my academic career. (The fact that I could not afford it also played a part in this.) But this self-sufficient attitude helped me in my teaching endeavors—compiling course material, exploring new perspectives of understanding, experimenting with lecture methods, etc.

Resonance

I was happily working for Bansal Sir. This job also helped me elevate the financial situation of my family. I was very hardworking, and Bansal Sir treated me as his son. He saw the spark of initiative and responsibility in me, which I have my parents to thank for. I was pretty content with my job then. So, all in all, it was going well.

But then, something was missing. I was not fulfilling my purpose of staying back in India. So far, I had only served myself, and maybe, a few of my students. I wanted to make a bigger impact on the world. I wanted to help create employment for people and enable more students to take up coaching and fix their careers.

So, in August 2000, I informed Bansal Sir that I would be leaving my job at his coaching center in nine months. I had never read about work ethics in a book or took a course. But I assured Bansal Sir to find a replacement for myself and train them before leaving the institute. Such were the values ingrained in me by my parents. At the time, Bansal Sir was a little disappointed. But he got my replacement, and we both worked together to train him to meet Bansal Sir's future requirements. So, when I finally left, there were no hard feelings between us.

And so, I started my venture called "Resonance" in 2001. I wanted to stand up to the promise that I had made to my mother at the time. I helped many capable people from my village to get jobs at Resonance. It wasn't nepotism in the strict sense; I only gave people jobs that they were capable of doing, and only to those who had a hunger to prove themselves but did not possess the means. Security guards, attendants, receptionists, and some teachers even; I could help all these people find employment. A few of their kids also got selected for IITs and top medical colleges. So, in a way, I could enable them to support their kids' education as well. I did not have much money saved up for it. I only had my experience, vigor, and a vision to fulfill the promise I made to my mother. We rented out a building, and our classes commenced with about 1000 students.

The vision for Resonance

The vision behind the name Resonance was inspired by the phenomenon of resonance, which is a crucial concept in Physics. But broadly, it signified the resonance of the thoughts between a student and a teacher, which is an even more critical factor. When we started out, we were, "Resonance, where you will be in resonance with IIT-JEE." We offered classroom coaching in Kota only for JEE at the time. But as we broadened our course sphere, I changed our motto to "Educating for a better tomorrow".

What drew people to us was that we did not only accept students who were already brilliant. We even took in those who were unclear about their studies and were still struggling a little. We helped them reach their goals. I used to take classes when not even a single teacher was ready to take, like a night at 10 o'clock batch.

Our results for the first year were not as impressive as the other classes in total number and ranks. But given the student pool that we had, we were very optimistic about what we had achieved. The growth was good, but the results weren't. People were making fun of us, and Bansal Classes looked like a giant in front of our small initiative.

Eventually, we started our junior division to groom students from 9th/10th grade and produce students who are capable of fetching higher ranks. This bought their trust in us. We started our distance learning and test series program after learning that our notes were being pirated to other classes.

As we gained more popularity, we expanded to about 15 buildings across Kota and started getting in more students every year. Although we were never the first preference, we did get a bunch of good students too, and they fetched us excellent results. In 2005, we started a center in Jaipur and eventually in Bhopal, Indore, etc. Now, we have centers all over India and conduct courses in various fields in commerce and arts as well.

The path ahead

My goal at Resonance has always been to adapt to the needs of the students. That is what keeps our institute running. We have continuous feedback rounds from students, and we closely monitor their progress throughout their journey. I have been training new professors since I started Resonance. Now, we run a very comprehensive Faculty Training Program for which we recruit fresh graduates from IITs/NITs, etc., and national-level recruitment tests.

We always had competitors in this industry. Our customer focus and a feedback-driven system have separated us from them. We always focused less on marketing and more on developing the product. In a way, I built up this institute for students like me, who need a channel for their passion for studies.

Coaching is often referred to as a money minting machine that deals in students' futures. But what the critics fail to see is the discipline and dedication that goes into facilitating smooth learning for all of these students. During the birth of three of my children, when my wife was in the hospital, my parents were taking care of her, and I was taking lectures. There are no holidays; there are no shortcuts. Planning papers and evaluating each and every student's potential is no meager feat.

Chapter 4

Richest Indian in the World

Gururaj Deshpande: Founder Deshpande Foundation

Desh is one of the most down-to-earth persons you can come across. Building one of the biggest Deep tech companies globally, Desh was an inspiration for a whole generation of Entrepreneurs, not just from IIT, but the whole of India. Even after accumulating a net worth above $7Bn in the 2000s, his living standards didn't change. After building such huge organizations, Desh started shifting his resources, time, and intelligence to give back to the scientific community and develop India. The most impressive thing about him was that he maintained his calm even after the bubble burst when chaos was everywhere and the firm's net worth was dropping. The reason for which, he says, "My net worth doesn't define my lifestyle."

The Fortunate Accidents

My time at IIT Madras was between the years 1968 to 1973. We never dedicated two or three years of our lives just to get into IIT back in those times. We only got to know about the IITs through hearsay.

I never thought I would go to IIT before I actually did. It was not as exciting back then as it is now. I learned about the entrance exams through one of my friends and decided to give it a shot. Then one day, a letter arrived at my father's office, calling me for an interview at IITM. A friend told him that it's tough to get into an IIT, so I should take up the opportunity.

Out went the telegram to my uncle's place, where I was staying at that time: "Start immediately." Purposefully short, as there was a word limit to these things. So off I went to Chennai (Madras) with much encouragement from my father.

Though my father had a decent job as a government labor commissioner, I attended a small Kannada medium school due to the transferable nature of his job. Compared to my school, the Chennai campus felt like a vast ocean. Meeting people from different states of India almost felt like meeting foreigners, each carrying their own cultural quirks. It was an eye-opening experience in many ways, where every day, I came across new ideas and mindsets. The first couple of months were admittedly overwhelming, as everyone there was brilliant, and the scenario was very competitive. Soon, I managed to learn to look past, and with time shed my inhibitions and embraced the richness of experience.

Back in those times, campus life meant weekly classes followed by camaraderie. My classmates were into western movies and all kinds of music, which I never had an opportunity to be exposed to earlier in my life. I wasn't even privy to the concept of entrepreneurship. There was just one thought that guided my actions—In life, if and when I got to do something, I would give my best to it. This quality, I believe, opened many doors for me throughout my career.

After B.Tech, I got placed at Telco systems as a trainee with a salary of 500 rupees a month, which was considered a big thing given the times. We had a Visiting Professor from Canada— Professor Gauri Shankar. While he was teaching us a course, he suggested that I try and apply to colleges in Canada because there were already many people going to the USA. He helped me with the names of a few universities. I followed his advice, applied, and ended up getting accepted with a full-paid scholarship. However, I still had the position at Telco, so I asked Gauri Shankar for advice again. He told me that "Telco will always be here. You should make the most of this new opportunity. Even if you don't settle there, it will expand your horizons." And that is the story of how I ended up in Canada.

The Teaching Tangent

After I did my Master's in Electrical Engineering, my advisor took a sabbatical and went to Australia. After my Master's, I wanted to return to India as I was feeling pretty homesick by then. At that time, my professor suggested that I stay back and fill in for him at the University of New Brunswick in Fredericton. It was undoubtedly an excellent opportunity for me to earn in dollars and gain experience.

So, I decided to teach for a year and realized I loved it. I also got voted as one of the best professors in the university. At that point, I felt convinced that, if anything, I should become a teacher-researcher. However, one could not become a researcher-teacher without a Ph.D. So, I ended up doing a Ph.D. in Data Communications from the Faculty of Engineering & Applied Sciences at Queen's University in Ontario, Canada.

Serendipitous Encounters

Peter Brackett was the Vice President of a start-up in Toronto called ESE Corporation. His company had developed modems that could operate at 9600 bits per second, which was impressive for that time, but the company had not been doing well financially. So, he left and came to teach at Queen's University. It so happened that around the same time, Motorola came in and bought that little struggling company in Toronto and offered Peter to go back and assume the post of Head of Engineering.

I completed my Ph.D. about four months after Peter left. One day, he called me up and said, "Hey Desh, why don't you come and join me in my venture. We could use your expertise." I had much respect for Peter, and hence immediately I agreed to join his 20 people garage operation, which was now a part of Motorola. Over the next four years, 1980-84, we went from 20 people to 400 people and evolved as $100 million worth of business.

My wife, Jaishree, is also an IITM alumnus. She came to IITM in 1973, the year that I graduated. We got married in 1980 and moved from Toronto to Boston together in 1984. It took about three years for us to get a green card. I then decided to take the plunge and start my own business, with much encouragement and support from Jaishree.

Midas's Malady

The first company that I started was Coral Networks, which focused on manufacturing routers. There were only two or three venture capitalists in all of Boston in those days. They were cautious about investing and did so only when they were convinced that the entrepreneur was genuinely committed to the idea at hand. Those days it was difficult, almost impossible to raise money unless you went without a salary for at least one year. So, I gave up my job with Motorola and started on the entrepreneurial journey in 1987.

After a year, we got a $3 million check from a very reputed Venture Capitalist. Unfortunately, my partner and I had a difference of opinion on product development. He was more focused on product perfection while I prioritized market timing. He was the Senior Partner; he had connections. In contrast, I was a young guy, and at that, a foreigner. We had an equal number of shares, but he was the more senior Co-founder. We argued about our differences. We could not reconcile. I talked to Jaishree and told her that I would quit because I didn't want to stay there and keep saying, "I told you so." Jaishree supported my decision, and I found the courage to quit.

With time it was evident that I was right. He kept spending a lot of money. Finally, the company got bought by another company called SynOptics at a small price. The venture capitalists got their money back. My co-founder and I had invested $300 each to start the company. We got back $26. It was a reminder that, unlike Midas, not everything I touch will turn to gold. That was my first failure. Fortunately, I could walk out of that situation defeated but not demotivated.

Turning Tables

After Coral, I started Cascade Communications. In the late 1980s, I sensed an opportunity at Motorola when we were in the business of connecting computers. However, during those times, only private networks existed globally. We started connecting employees, branches, and eventually some client bases to establish communication within and outside the company. The network kept on expanding indefinitely and at an exponential rate. Networking went from connecting individual computers to connecting many computers within the company to connecting computers from different companies.

The advent of phone lines witnessed a similar trend. Initially, big companies used phones to connect their unit offices. They could not conceive of an individual phone that connects with every other phone in the world.

While starting Cascade, I felt that computers could follow the same trajectory as phones. If so, we would need a worldwide network to connect every computer in the world with each other. That network will no longer be private; it needs to be public.

Building large-scale public networks require scalable data switches. The existing leading Telecommunications Companies in the industry were building large phone switches and were adding token data switching capabilities to those switches. This made those switches very expensive and not very scalable.

The idea behind Cascade was to build dedicated data switches for public networks so that any user can connect to them in any way. This was an aspirational dream when I started, but fortunately, it worked out very well! The internet was right around the corner, and overwhelming market reception it was.

By 1997, we were carrying 80% of the internet backbone traffic.

Cascade happened to be the right thing arriving at the right time and was propelled with excellent execution with the support of a lot of capable people. It went public in 1994. We sold Cascade to Ascend Communications for $3.7 billion in 1997.

TiE

When I was the Head of TiE Boston, I used to mentor many emerging start-ups. I had the time and knowledge to be of tangible use to them. At that time, I met a couple of guys from MIT working on fiber optics. That led to Sycamore.

PoP!

Sycamore started in 1998. At that time leading data switching companies were spending billions of dollars to provide quality service for video and audio traffic with minimal bandwidth over the wide-area networks. Bandwidth was not only costly but also very cumbersome to sustain. For example, if someone wanted 1.5 Mbps from Boston to Chicago, it would take six months and cost tens of thousands of dollars every month. We gave a shot at trying to solve this problem and came up with a concept called intelligent optical network. This network enabled us to decrease the provisioning time from six months to six minutes in real-time. This was a huge hit. Also, the timing was perfect. Data traffic was exploding. We started shipping the product in the sixth quarter after starting the company. Our growth was explosive. Our quarterly growth was $10M, $20M, $30M, $60M, $90M, $120M, and $150M.

Sycamore went public in the seventh quarter after starting the company, and the company valuation shot up to $50B. Soon after that, the bubble burst, and the growth rate slowed down. We decided to adjust our business focus on optical switching and resized the company at that time.

Making a Difference

When I turned 50, my wife and I decided that we didn't want to be entrepreneurs anymore. We want to become enablers.

The entrepreneurial journey was unbelievable. Every year took me by surprise, and whenever I turned to look back, I realized I was doing things that I never knew I could do. Everyone who worked for our company shared the same feeling. It was such an exhilarating journey that we wanted to create similar opportunities for hundreds of others through our Foundation. That is how Deshpande Foundation got started.

After Sycamore, I used to pick one company a year and get deeply involved with it. Typically, I would be the largest investor and Chairman of the company. That was a fun engagement. However, I found it to be somewhat limiting. Therefore, we started using our Foundation's resources to enable many entrepreneurs and not to get involved with a specific company. I joined the Board of MIT in 2000 and started the Deshpande Centre for Technological Innovation soon after.

Looking Back

I have always tried to keep my life simple. Not because I was making any sacrifices. Instead, it freed me to do the things that I really wanted to do. I see many of my successful friends trapped in a place with a lot of money but no time to live their lives. Added income will always bring added complexities. I think simplicity is more for natural, experiential contentment than an abstract glorified virtue. That's the best way to optimize happiness. When one can strike that right balance naturally, there can be no other way of doing it.

My in-laws and parents were reluctant to let me go for another start-up after the first one failed. And by all means, they meant well. They were very concerned about me. They did not want to see me get hurt again. However, one needs an unyielding, indomitable conviction to continue down the path that one has chosen for oneself. Real strength lies in owning up to what one wants in life and doing justice to each effort to achieve it.

I hope that in the next five years, we will start seeing the impact of the work we are doing at the Deshpande Foundation in India, the USA, and Canada. We are hoping that we will enable many people to get the opportunity to live that exciting life they always wanted for themselves, a truly worthwhile life that is beyond their dreams.

Brief Chronicles 1

Prashant Pitti
IIT Madras, BTech – Elec 2005
Co-Founder, EaseMyTrip.com

EaseMyTrip is the second largest and only profitable travel portal in India. EaseMyTrip is truly an exception, as the only consumer-tech company globally that is bootstrapped, listed, and has crossed the $1 billion mark. The company has no debt, is cash-rich, and is growing rapidly.

My time at IIT Madras was one of the best experiences, where I was able to learn the real strength of determination, resilience, and teamwork. Further, it completely changed my perspective towards technology.

I learned an important lesson at IIT Madras: Focus on building your USP (Unique Selling Proposition) and not be a part of something that just exists. There will be extreme challenges where all the odds may be against you, but your determination to stay away from mediocrity and achieve something unique should always be your goal.

I have learned a lot from Ashok Jhunjhunwala Sir and other faculty members, as they truly inspired me during my time at IIT Madras. Ashok Sir's immense contribution towards technology and the importance of having a facility like IIT Madras Research Park is genuinely memorable and encouraging to date.

Chapter 5

Manufacturing the Country Ahead

Amrit Acharya: Zetwerks

After years of work experiences at MNCs like Bosch, Avaya, and ITC, he went abroad to pursue his post-graduation in business and even worked there for a couple of years, only to realize that India was where he could bring about some real change. Amrit, along with his friend from IITM, Srinath Ramakkrushnan, got together and went around numerous roadblocks and pivots while navigating the manufacturing marketplace of India to create a unicorn—Zetwerks.

To say the least, Amrit's story is one hell of a rollercoaster. From being a branch changer in the first year to getting a 6 GPA in his fourth year as a Sponsorship Headfor Saarang (Cultural Fest of IITM), he has seen it all. From an assistant manager in a factory in the town of Guntur to the Founder of one of the largest manufacturing service firms in India, he has also been it all.

How a boy from Odisha went on to raise a billion dollars for his start-up is not a matter of chance, nor is it a matter of fate. It is the outcome of years of industry experience paired with the desire to make a difference. Here is his story.

Life before campus

I'm originally from Bhubaneswar, Odisha. Some of us living in metropolitan cities take for granted the accessibility and amenities that are still lacking in other, less prominent parts of the country. Although I loved growing up in Odisha, I also felt the need to leave the place as soon as possible. It was like when a bird had to leave its nest. JEE came along as an excellent opportunity to do that. Despite my parents' persistence, I went to an IIT that was far away from home. I wanted to spread my wings and explore the world around me.

The College Compendium

My first year was atypical of my time at IIT Madras because I initially got into the Biotechnology branch. Even though I liked the field, it didn't feel like the best match for me. So, I spent most of my first year studying to change my branch to Electrical Engineering. Although this gave me a great GPA, I still missed out on many things that my new campus had to offer. I had not used much of my newly acquired freedom.

So, I spent the rest of my time in college diversifying my interests and making the most out of my time. When I was in my second year, I won a competition in Shaastra (Technical Festival of IITM), which landed me an internship at Bosch. I spent my whole summer in Bosch, understanding the company. After that, I went to an exchange program at NYU in my third year. In my fourth year, I was a Coordinator for Saarang for sponsorship and public relations.

Although admittedly, my exploration did reflect on my grade, which went from 9.4 to 8, then to 7 and 6 in the fourth year, during my stint as a core group member for Saarang, I was happy that I could pursue my interests. Thankfully, the line of work that I went in did not pay much attention to grades. My biggest takeaway from college was the opportunity to pursue my interests and make many friends along the way.

NYU Semex

The semester exchange program was not exactly a popular option at my time because it would take away six months of your college, and it was not very clear what was to be gained from it. But you never know what you might end up with when you take up something new. I went to NYU with a hostel mate of mine, Srinath. We ended up becoming great friends there. We eventually went on to build a company together.

When I was at NYU, there was an internship drive going on in the Institute. I applied for an internship in Singapore, but as fate had it, the market crash took place that same year, and I could not make it there. Looking for an alternative, I started reaching out to the Alumni ecosystem.

But one of my seniors took me aside and showed me, "Look at your CV and look at this other guy's CV who has 20 years of experience. How are you going to compete with that? You need to build a stronger CV to land this."

This was humiliating but not unfair. I realized that no matter how much pedigree you bring with your degree, you cannot compete with experience. So, I struggled a lot to get an internship in my third-year summer and finally got it at Avaya.

Core at Saarang

I'm not surprised that many of the entrepreneurs from the Institute have been sponsorship coordinators at Saarang. It's one of the few platforms in college where you get to interact with the real world and with real money. In 2010, when I became a core group member, we had just exited a recession, and nobody wanted to spend money. In spite of that, we were able to pull it off somehow. It's funny to think about a college student asking Vodafone for sponsorship for a college festival and not getting thrown out.

The place taught me sales, and the most significant thing you learn in sales is humility. Many people look down on sales as a job because it's not nearly as "sexy" as some of the more sophisticated titles. But the skills required for sales are so vast and versatile. In a world of commerce, if you know how to sell, you know how to survive.

How I met my wife

My time at Saarang is also what made me cross paths with my wife. We were both on the same team. She was two years my junior. Even after graduation, I would come back to campus to meet her. She was my real inspiration for becoming an entrepreneur. She took the initiative of starting a magazine during her college days. Ultimately, it did not work out. But the fact that she put up a fight even though people around her did not understand her reasons and were reluctant to accept her ideas was a great inspiration to me.

Life at ITC

In my final year, I ended up getting placed at ITC as an assistant manager. McKinsey used to hire just a couple of students back then, and it was BCG's first year to hire from our campus. ITC offered a fantastic package of Rs10 lakhs. Srinath also got into ITC with me, and we grew more aligned in our thoughts and ideas while working together.

When I got posted in the Guntur district, the first thought which came to my mind was to drop it. What could I accomplish here?

But I decided to give it a shot for a month, and it was possibly one of the best decisions of my life.

My boss at ITC, Sanjeev, was the chief executive of the division where I was working. He made a very prominent impression on me. To date, I still look up to him as my mentor, and he is also one of the angel investors in my company. He taught us to run a team and how to take any job hands-on.

My job at ITC was to build a new factory. I was quite surprised that they would entrust a fresh graduate with such a big responsibility. Although it was unusual, I was still handling hundreds of crores worth of spending, working with 200-300 suppliers, and managing over 1000 workers. I was part of a small team managing all these tasks. In hindsight, it was an entrepreneurial experience. I worked in Guntur for a year and moved to Mysore, only to return to Guntur after two years to report to Sanjeev again, this time as his Chief of Staff. Whatever we did from thereon directly aligned with what we are doing today.

I started out thinking that I would work at ITC for just a month but ended up doing it for four years. But after gaining many growth experiences, it finally came to a point where I could not imagine myself going further in this line of work. All my other friends lived in cities like Delhi and Mumbai, and their lives were very different. Over here, we had very little to do. We made money, but we didn't have much of anything to spend it on. 80% of my salary went into my savings, which helped me later. I decided to pursue my higher education overseas.

Shifting Shores

I realized that my learning had become relatively dormant and that I had been living in a bubble for quite some time. I applied to a few schools and managed to get into Berkeley.

At Berkeley, I was presented with two choices—a generalist or a specialist. A book called "Range: Why Generalists Triumph in a Specialized World" talks about what it means to be both of those things and what sort of roles they take up in the world. I did a bit of soul searching and realized that I love problem-solving, but I don't have that kind of patience, which would drive me to do one thing for a long time. I need variety in the problems I help solve, which took me back to my time at ITC. My boss gave me enough freedom to make all the decisions I wanted. I was having so much fun doing it that getting paid for it was just an upside for me. Entrepreneurship should be like that.

I went through a period of confusion when I was in B-School. I tried my hands at coding and dedicated six months to learn how to make apps. But I realized that although I could do this work, I would never be at the top of my game at it. My forte had always been problem-solving, and I was already pretty good at it. Life is not a linear journey, but we can always look back and connect the dots. The narrative was not straightforward, but it was clear to me what I had to do now.

The USA experience

My time at Berkeley made me realize the stark differences between Indian Institutes and US universities. Apart from the course structure itself, the environment was another major factor that weighed in.

In hindsight, I would not have gone abroad to do an MBA had I known then what I know now. I believe that you can learn business only by doing business in the field and not by studying about it in a classroom. Many things taught to me in the B-school were different from what I saw in the real world. I think it's challenging for one educational model to keep up with the immensely fast-paced world of business, where all the real action happens.

In Berkeley, I discovered that a lot more focus was placed on the individual as compared to India. There was much more freedom for an individual to pursue his/her path. Although I was doing an MBA, I had the option to take up some engineering courses as a part of my degree too.

Most of my time at Berkeley was spent in its engineering school, talking to many Ph.D. and Master's students. Being a generalist, I wanted to connect with more specialists and see if I could find the right fit with someone to start something together.

I finished my MBA there in two years and worked at Mckinsey for a year. After that, I joined a small firm in the Bay Area. Although my work was not related to core, my engineering background helped me. It gave an entirely new approach to my problem-solving. Rather than looking at it as one big problem, it enabled me to view it as ten minor problems.

I spent around three years in the US and six months in Australia. But after three years abroad, my wife and I started discussing our future in this country. We still had to apply for immigration, and it was unclear whether we would get it. If I did end up getting it, I would have to work at Mckinsey for years to come because that's how the system works. You cannot change jobs that easily.

We had to ask ourselves, what is it that we wanted to do? What do we enjoy while we are here, and what are we missing out on? After much contemplation, we decided to leave the US because we could not live our life with all the restrictions that came with living there. And so, my time in the Bay Area, though excellent, came to an end. We packed our bags and went back home to India. We had no plans and no jobs! We just had one thing in our minds—we wanted to start a venture of our own and run it on our own terms.

Come to think of it, I could have started up straight out of ITC. I was professionally ready for it. But Berkeley gave me the space for a lot of personal growth, and its environment broadened my horizons. It showed me the path towards what I could achieve.

Log kya kahenge (Gosh! How would people react?)

Sharanya and I moved back in January of 2018. We wanted to get married before December that same year. So, my dad gave me a deadline. Get a job by December, or he'd have to introduce me as 'Unemployed' during the marriage ceremony.

Moving back to India was a big challenge. I spent the first nine months without a job, something which we would not have survived had I not saved up so much during my time at ITC.

My mother was very supportive when I was thinking about starting up.

She started her own company when she was 58, and I guess I inherited her entrepreneurial spirit. She told me that I could take as much time as I needed with my new company. But on the other hand, I had a deadline to keep with Dad. So, the two of them together were the perfect combination of inspiration and support for me to start up.

But most importantly, I could not have done it if Sharanya wasn't there to support me at every step of the way. When I came back to India, I applied for a bunch of jobs and even managed to get one. But she told me we did not come back to India to get another job. That statement held so much power that it energized me to work for nine months without a salary.

The makings of Zetwerk

After coming back to India, I got back in touch with Srinath. We exchanged thoughts, and serendipitously, both of us agreed upon the idea of starting up something of our own. To understand the problem statement we were working on, I needed to recall all of the learnings that I had picked up during my time at ITC.

Companies like GE (General Electric Company is an American multinational conglomerate incorporated in New York City) are fundamentally into manufacturing. There is a design team and a procurement team.

The structure of these companies is such that 20-30% of manufacturing, which is very difficult to make, relies on third-party partners, which are small businesses. One of them being the one Srinath's family used to run.

These are the small entrepreneurs who have small factories; they take in the designs usually made with software like AutoCAD. They have the machinery and the workforce, through which they convert that design into a fully-fledged product. Now, there is no data about the capacity and qualifications of these manufacturers.

Also, unlike the retail businesses, the businesses that we buy from have no retail price; the price must be met based on the willingness to pay in proportion to the services procured. In the B2C sector, you can place an order online and receive the package within a week with the invoice. You also get to track the order step by step from storage to your doorstep. But in the B2B world, it's completely different. The transactions are carried out over a range of months, and there is no organized feedback system in place to tackle these challenges.

So, to make things easier in the B2B supply chain, we came up with a software tool that enables one to interact with their suppliers. Many more prominent firms were reluctant to take up this service because they said they had to convince their higher-ups who sat in foreign offices. They did not get to make these decisions in India. But at the same time, they asked us if they could use the software's abilities to find new suppliers.

Taking off with a pivot

This was where we came up with our first pivot. Instead of offering a self-service product like software, we decided to go deeper and provide an entire marketplace. We found that that's what people primarily used the software for. We worked on that for six months and finally established a network that connected the suppliers with the businesses. So, if a firm came to this network, it would help them find the right supplier out of the thousands listed on the platform. There are many variables to consider. For example, the price, the transportation distance, manufacturability, and the extent of the supplier's capabilities. For this matchmaking, we charge a small marketplace commission.

By January 2019, although we were getting many orders, not many orders were delivered because suppliers in India lacked the ecosystem to support fulfillment. We soon realized that customers specifically in India wanted us to go one level deeper and do all of this work for them. We will take the order, locate the suppliers, and ensure your product is delivered on time. We will give you complete visibility as to what's happening on a day-to-day basis. When we got this comprehensive model up and running, that's when our business took off.

We had built a marketplace for the manufacturing industry. On the demand side, we worked with large corporations that typically focused on industrial projects. We were helping these designers convert their vision into reality. Through our technology, we could give them a real-time status report of the completion of their work. Whether a supplier has received an order, started the manufacturing process, bought the raw material, or finished the painting job, our buyers could see whether the product is 70% ready or 90%.

We brought many layers to this, like work-in-progress photos, to provide as much transparency as possible. Today, we have around 250-odd customers and 2000-odd suppliers in India. Our company enables creators to keep on creating and manufacturers to keep on producing without thinking about the gap between the two because that's where we come in.

In 2019, we financially grew 20-fold in one year. In 2020, even though it has been a pretty tough year for the entire country and the world, we still grew three times, touching 1000 crores in revenue, and we are expecting the growth to be at the same speed for the upcoming year.

At a macro level, we can see that India is becoming a pivotal supplier in the world market. Due to the jarring impact of Covid-19, the international companies that used to rely primarily on east Asian countries like China, Taiwan, Vietnam, and Korea want to explore more options and diversify their suppliers. India is the only other country that can offer it at this scale.

Today, 10% of our business is International. Most of them are first-time buyers in India and want to explore India. But it gets complicated to do so for a bunch of reasons.

There are many complexities to overcome, the first being the knowledge barrier, and the second being credibility. They have no way to ascertain which manufacturers can handle the requirements of their consignment.

This, again, is where we come into the picture. We communicate with the suppliers and tell them that we will scan the entire market for you. We already have all the supplier details and capabilities in our database. We also have records of the past projects implemented by our suppliers, which we share with the new ones for them to understand the situation better. This saves them a whole lot of work and time.

Prospects

A lack of formal credit is a problem in India, and that is something we wanted to fix for the entire manufacturing ecosystem. Often, our customers tell us that they would like us to integrate our model in other countries. We are also considering expanding to other markets around the world. There, we would get to interact with an entirely different customer pool and test international waters.

Chapter 6

Back to the Future

Dr. Satya Chakravarthy: Co-founder, The ePlane Company

Dr. Chakravarthy is a professor of Aerospace engineering at IIT Madras, but is unlike any professor you will ever come across. Along with his academic duties, he has Co-founded three Start-ups in the Deep Tech space and headed the National Centre for Combustion Research and Development (NCCRD).

He is also unconventional in his entrepreneurial journey, as he started on this path after hitting his fifties. You can call it half a century's worth of experience and vision which he has over his younger counterparts.

Starting up this "late" brings its own set of challenges too, but he tackles them with a pioneering grace. Let's hear his legacy starting from his early college days.

The college conveyor belt

When we were students, we were not so comfortable with the idea of entrepreneurship. Even today, as a teacher at an IIT, I think that the mentality of students is very risk-averse. Much too early on in their lives, they are concerned about what their future will look like. They look to make "smart" decisions that would minimize any risk of failure. This is good to a certain extent, but I think it limits many possibilities.

The fact that these students gave two or more years of their lives writing JEE shows a significant degree of risk mitigation already ingrained in their heads. In my opinion, we would be better off as a country if we didn't have this so-called illusion of a secure life after engineering. Instead of signing up for a conveyor belt that takes us to the future, students should seek out their paths and establish themselves in the world. When I was a student, the trend was to get into IIT, get tinkered, molded, refined, and then boxed out with an IITian label and an export quality stamp, ready to be shipped out. At least, that was what was happening at the time.

The situation today is better in terms of the variety of opportunities available to students. The start-up culture in the country is growing for the better, and there are many opportunities to find mentors and investors to give your start-up the edge.

At IITM

A lot of the decisions I made in college reflected my entrepreneurial streak. For example, since I got into the Aerospace branch, I could get a good CGPA and change my unit to mechanical engineering, which was more sought after. I did come up second in my class, which would allow me to do so. But I stopped and thought for a moment. If I left Aerospace for mechanical, I would be 26th in the Mechanical branch, which left me with a relatively lower CPI. Alternatively, if I let the guy ahead of me change his branch, I would be the first in my branch, and I could maintain a good CPI throughout my degree. This would get me into the Georgia Institute of Technology later on. So, foresight is always an excellent tool to keep in your arsenal as an entrepreneur.

After IIT

It was customary to go and study abroad once after IIT, which is what most of us did. My classmates and I were a bunch of nerds, and we were pretty good at being nerds. And anything you are good at, you should be proud about, and so we were. We were always thinking about what we learned in class and applying it in real life. We used to come back to hostels and develop our ideas and have hearty discussions on the same. These are some things that are very rare among teenagers these days.

And it was not like we were missing out on a lot of things either. We were delighted with the college's exposure and were having a good time learning from our teachers. A lot of us also made up our minds to come back here and teach. I used to wonder how IITM would accommodate so many professors for one subject. Would they agree to take all of us back? (At that time, our branch size was 14, and the number of faculty members was 18.)

One more reason was that in 1991, it was just about the time before liberalization happened in India. I think IIT professors were making good salaries. We felt that all you had to do was go abroad, get a PhD. and land a lecturership here. The universities abroad were also more than ready to take up IITians. It was the smoothest journey we could hope for. So, again, we had mapped our stay on the conveyor belt.

Once we went abroad, though, everyone's mind changed except for mine.

Life at Georgia Tech

I was into rocket propulsion and combustion at Georgia Tech with the world-famous rocket scientist for my advisor, Prof. Ed Price. He was probably the oldest rocket scientist alive in the world at the time. He was already 70 years old.

Interestingly, on the very day that I joined, there was a Ph.D. student who was just leaving after completing his Ph.D. with Prof. Price. He advised me to complete my Ph.D. as soon as possible. Because the guy was already 70, he'd suffered a heart attack at 52, followed by the usual ailments accompanying old age, it would be in my best favor to complete my Ph.D. while he was still alive.

I liked Price a lot. But under him, I worked like a mad dog so that I was able to finish my Ph.D. in just four years. Despite this, he still had a lot of kicks in him when I finished. I worked so hard at that time that working my ass off became second nature to me. It helped me in the times in the future when I needed it.

Life at IITM as the professor building NCCRD

Many other friends started making other plans when they went to the US and decided not to return. I came back to IIT Madras to teach as a professor. And yet, I was not the professor I thought I would be as a naive student. I grew on to be very ambitious and hardworking. I clocked in many more hours than others and was very diligent. I was always busy, working on some project I had undertaken and was very productive most of the time. This landed me a few awards here and there and allowed me to set up some excellent laboratories in the institute.

I was the founder and head of the NCCRD (National Centre for Combustion Research & Development).

When we presented our proposal to the Secretary of the Department of Science and Technology, he gave one look at it and said, "Your proposal looks like it is for a museum. Where are the operations?" He asked me to explain what we were planning to do in the laboratory. And I explained it to him in person. He heard me out and told me these are the things he expects to see in the proposal.

He told us that since he gave us the money, there is no point in the proposal if it does not highlight the use of all this equipment. He continued to list out all the issues in the draft and instructed us on how a proposal is written. I was amazed by that display of understanding and patience. We got back to work again and articulated the grand challenges that needed to be formulated for this lab.

Once we finished the setup, we began to get spectacular results. Results of these kinds were unprecedented anywhere in the world. We were even filing patents based on them. After writing many papers, attending conferences, and propagating our findings, we got a lot of recognition for our work there. We emerged as world leaders in this line of research. I'm delighted that I got to be at the forefront of this exciting endeavor.

I was at the peak of my profession as a professor. But I still felt like something was missing. All the recognition and renown did not satisfy me like I had hoped it would.

The Startup Professor

I wanted my work to see the light of day in practical devices within the course of my life instead of just lying around as patents and papers. When we talk about pushing this technology into usable devices, it essentially means that we have to go back to the industry we have been working with. I would be working with GE, Siemens, Rolls Royce, or any engine companies in Aerospace.

It's not like I did not interact with these companies before thinking of doing my own thing. But through my interaction with them, I realized something. They are market leaders and are at the frontier of their industries. I had a different view because I solved a problem they'd faced for the last 20 years. It's not so easy for them to listen. It comes down to institutional ego. How can they listen to Satya, a professor who has been cut off from the industry for the better part of his career?

They, of course, did not say all this to my face. They would come up with some pretext like manufacturing limitations or lack of resources. But despite all this, I thank them for their rejection because my exasperation in convincing them made me consider starting up on my own.

But what does being an entrepreneur mean?

I used my experience as a researcher and broke the process down into levels. So, the first problem in front of me was to see how my technology could fit into a product that could be useful. It's like having a hammer in your hand and looking for nails to hit.

The next question you have to ask is, "Who needs this product?" Because having the technology, you have to think of making a product. And after you complete the product, you have to figure out who will use it. Here comes the question for the makers. So, where does the product-market fit lie? What pain of the customer are you alleviating? So, all the jargon about entrepreneurship, customer discovery, customer exploration, logistics, etc., all began to come to me.

Disruptive Innovation

I read the book The Innovator's Dilemma; it blew my mind. Not a week goes by when I don't think about what it said. It mentions a concept called Disruptive Innovation.

When completed correctly, disruptive technology can be better than mainstream technology. The challenge is that you have to emerge through an uncharted market, one that the metric of the mainstream industry has not already marked.

This will initially go unnoticed by the industry leaders because it would be beneath their radar. The mainstream industry will continue to look after existing customers and not go looking for potential ones.

But you end up making excellent margins within that consumer base. This creates a kind of vacuum at the bottom, where you position yourself and grow with this new market you have identified. After that, you keep improving your product and get to the point where you are not only as good as the existing competitors but also are filling in the gaps they overlooked.

So, you're sort of edging them up and out by attacking them from below. This beautiful framework precisely captures how new companies replace old ones. All this is almost like corporate law. When I understood this, I started believing that it's okay to make inferior products, provided you can identify a market stronghold.

My first start-up, Agnikul, is making a mini rocket for taking sub-100 kg class satellites at a much lower cost than what a giant rocket will do by putting them through wait times.

My second start-up, Aestrovilos, made a micro gas turbine, cheaper and more long-lasting than a diesel Genset, but inferior to a gas turbine of its class.

And finally, with E-plane, we are designing hybrid-electric planes for short-range intercity travels to redefine urban mobility. Our concentration was on autonomous and sustainable technology.

With all these ventures, we focused on creating the product for the market and not bothering about the conventional industry since our area of expertise was uncharted.

You can grow in new markets, attack them from below and age them up and out. This is the method to the madness, as the cliche goes.

The runway for the Plane

Early October 2016, I got this video from one of my acquaintances, an alumnus of IIT. It's a 53-minute video by a guy called Tony Sabir. He is a Stanford professor and thought leader. He has been evangelizing electric mobility and solar. This was a video that he had presented in 2016 March at a conference in Oslo.

It's 1900 in New York. They have a parade full of horse-drawn carriages, and there, he asks you to identify a motorcar. Following this, he shows you a picture of an Easter parade in 1913. There were cars everywhere. Now, he asks you to identify carriages. His point was in about 13 years, there was such a massive transformation that the entire set of horses and carriages disappeared and were replaced by motor cars.

In 1900, they couldn't have predicted what would happen in the next 13 years. Tony's essential point was that in 2016, he would show a lot of data that was essentially expecting that by 2030, we will not have any combustion cars at all and only electric engine cars. He made a lot of intermediate steps to it, one of them being that in 2020, the cost of an electric vehicle will start dropping below the IC engine car. In 2025, automobile companies will stop making IC engine cars. By 2030, everybody would have even abandoned their IC engine cars and switched to electric vehicles. This is the roadmap.

Similarly, he said that by 2017, solar would hit grid parity, which it did in India and the rest of the world. At the end of this 53-minute video, I was shaken.

Thinking, 'What the heck am I doing trying to set up this world's largest combustion centre when cars become electric and thermal power will be replaced by solar?'

This means that most of the population will stop burning up fuels, and the primary frontiers of combustion would be aerospace propulsion.

I realized that planes would be the next thing to be attacked and encroached upon by electrification. That night, the epiphany of designing an electric aircraft came to me.

Starting up E-plane

When you go to conferences, no industry leaders are talking about this. They are in denial about the change in terms of electrification.

After watching this video, my question was, will I spend the rest of my career in denial and continue to get encroached upon and become irrelevant?

No. I knew I had to embrace the change and get on the bandwagon. But what does that imply? Should I also set out to make electric cars—something the mainstream industry has been trying for years? No.

But if I make electric planes, I can be at the frontier of that line of innovation. There were, of course, people already doing this, but not on a vast scale. Regardless, I had a lot to learn from them. I found a lot of papers that were being presented at conferences. I also interacted with a set of people that were continuously publishing things.

April of 2017 was when we started ideating the Plane. We directly jumped into the design for the aircraft but realized that we did not have the funds that we needed.

So, we decided to start with drones, which were relatively easier to make. We concentrated our efforts on making efficient delivery drones. But many people were doing drones. So, we wanted to specialize our drones for longer distances. We finally had our prototype ready by 2019. But we came across many regulatory hurdles while trying to commercialize it. Then, we realized that we should drop this endeavor and work on what we originally had in mind. Businesses always take unexpected turns this way. It's as crucial to know when to stop as when to push ahead.

With our experience on the drone, we could go ahead, make the Plane, and keep it within the regulatory realm.

But that is a boundary we will have to keep pushing as there is no shortcut to reliability in technology. I have developed patience over the years, and it has helped me a lot throughout my entrepreneurial journey.

We are in the process of raising a seed funding of a million dollars. By mid-2022, we expect the prototype of our two-seater taxi to fly. So, this is the roadmap that we have for the E-plane.

Agnikul

The story of how Agnikul came to be is also very pivotal in my career.

While working at the Combustion Centre, we started working with GE on 3D metal printed combustors for gas turbine engines used in aircraft applications. These require fuel injection that will burn at high temperatures, and high-pressure air enters the combustor over extended periods. We needed to ensure the structural integrity and longevity of the material. We were continuously conducting tests on models, and our work at the Centre gained a lot of momentum.

That's also when Shreenath, the CEO of Agnikul, contacted me and asked to have an online meeting with me. So, sometime in the middle of 2017, he pitched the idea of making an orbital launch vehicle in India, working in collaboration with our Centre. He admitted later that I was one of many people he contacted, and I was the only one who agreed.

When Shreenath came in October, we incorporated the company.

The funny thing is that I never went in to check whether Shreenath had any background in Rocket Propulsion. I saw his drive for the vision, and that was enough for me to decide. For entrepreneurs, that leap of faith is significant. You never know for sure whether or not something will work out. You need to believe in the vision and trust that you will make it through the process.

Investors are like IITians in a way. They try to mitigate risks to the maximum extent possible. What they don't realize is that—that sort of thinking just restricts innovation. They often ask irrelevant questions. For example, in E-plane, Pranjal does not know how to make planes, which did not end up mattering. We can always bring in consultants and experts in the industry. The question is, who will get the ball rolling and get the work done?

They look for the team having the right kind of background. If they find that the team is good, only then will they put in their money. One of our first investors that Shreenath got in touch with admitted that I was the only reason he was willing to put in the capital. That was a big responsibility, but in deep tech, you need so much more than just a tech background, and people don't appreciate the kind of work that goes into it. It was important to me to live up to my reputation and give it my best from what I had to offer.

We had difficulty raising money in the first couple of rounds, but we are doing well now. The next fundraising round will hopefully be the last one before our first launch. Once we raise the next round of funding, we can go towards a suborbital launch sometime in 2022.

In Deep Tech, one has to realize that the point of entry is that if you have failures, you try again. Our investors are beginning to understand this and can understand the risks much better now. One of our investors asked me, "Suppose I give you a million dollars and you fail, would you come back and ask me for 10 million dollars to fix it or just one more million?"

I replied, "Just another million would do."

That is the kind of failure risk analysis that we will have to go by. So, the point is, if we fail in 2022, maybe we will. We will succeed in 2023. The audacity to take up these kinds of problems to solve themselves seems to motivate many people.

You have to learn from the failure to succeed the next time. So, considering that, I think we are on the path to success, even if we happen to fail in the middle.

Final Remarks

Only a couple of professors are running with new ideas in Deep Tech. We don't have entrepreneurs who are picking it up. So, we face the following problem—if I come up with the next big tech idea, which has a significant economic impact, do I have enough entrepreneurs to take it up? Or are all the young entrepreneurs running behind quickie problems like E-commerce? That's where our current challenges are. We need entrepreneurial students who can pick it up and run with it as a long-term enterprise.

Therefore, here, we are developing the basics of how to do entrepreneurship. Most of the Silicon Valley guys are people like Peter Thiel, who writes books about this; they haven't delved into Deep Tech spaces, which is extremely difficult to do and requires consistent and long-term efforts.

The kind of research happening at our Combustion Center does not occur anywhere else in the world. For people in India, it is difficult to digest that we have the best of XYZ technology. They always presume that the best is in some other country that has a more robust economy. But the economy, although an important tool, does not arouse innovation. It only enables it. We have to rid ourselves of this mentality that India is incapable of doing Deep Tech. With its resources and strength and a belief that it has the potential to be at the top of our industry, we can achieve it.

If it happens right next door, why can't it happen here? That is the sort of mindset entrepreneurs in the deep tech side need to foster.

Chapter 7

The Junglee Book

Anand Rajaraman: Founder—Junglee

Remember your class topper—the one who always aced all subjects, and you found yourself wondering whether to be impressed or annoyed? Anand was that student throughout college—a feat that got him the President of India Medal of excellence at IIT Madras.

This was far from the pinnacle of achievements for Anand. In many ways, he was the conventional academic, but in many ways, he wasn't. For example, he took a leave of absence from his Ph.D. at Stanford to start up with his batchmates!

Anand has broken his share of stereotypes as a student, as an entrepreneur, and later on, as a Venture Capitalist. Read on to discover his legacy.

College and Common rooms

One thing that is strikingly different now from how it used to be during my college time is the interaction between students. You see, although our hostel building was the same, Alak (Alakananda), there was no internet connection back then. Not even a wired connection. There was no Netflix. There was no streaming whatsoever. If you wanted to use a computer, you'd have to go to the lab.

Hence, most of my social life at college was spent in my hostel common room playing chess, table tennis, or the likes. I did not partake in any sport, but I was an avid spectator in most of the matches. At the time (maybe, even now), there used to be a great rivalry between Alak and Godavari. Some of the moments from cricket matches are still vivid in my memories. I used to play a little chess for the hostel team, but I didn't get very far with it.

Yes, I won the President of India Gold Medal (awarded to the student with the best academic record among those graduating at each convocation.) I was very passionate about my field of study and its subjects. But I was still unclear about what I wanted to do with that passion. Nevertheless, I was very focused on my academics, and yes, I ended up doing very well in that field. That said, I did have my share of fun in those four years. Hostel life taught me a lot of things about the world and myself. It was a fulfilling experience, but I knew I still had a long way to go from here.

Chalo Stanford

The job scenario for CSE in India was not very strong. It's changed so drastically over the past two decades. I did have an offer from one of these outsourcing companies in computer science, but it was evident that Stanford would be more enjoyable.

I will be honest with you. There was no great epiphany that told me that I needed to apply at Stanford or any of the colleges abroad at the time. It was like a ritual to apply to foreign universities after passing out from an IIT in those days. So, at that time, it was a no-brainer for me. I liked my field a lot and was good at it. And getting a higher education seemed like the right decision. So, I took it. I applied to some of the top colleges, and I got into Stanford. Stanford had the strongest and most exciting faculties at college.

I was pursuing a Ph.D. in Computer Science. You could see clear aspirational similarities in all the people studying there in IIT because we all fell through the same filter (JEE). I found it interesting when I came to Stanford because there were people from all over the world who were different. In IIT, most of the courses prescribed for us were compulsory, exempting the occasional electives that we had taken. But at Stanford, I had the liberty to pick any class that I wanted. The only thing I had to do was pick a faculty advisor at the end of my first year.

The ZOO and its Inmates

In the first year, we had this enormous office area in our building, which was called "the ZOO". The rationale behind that name was beyond me. But the people I shared that room with were unlike anyone I have known before. So, this was where we had our workstations set up, and we had some of our classes there.

My cubicle in The Zoo was next to Sergey Brin's (co-founder Google). This guy had always been the oddball eccentric genius. He had fascinating ideas, most of which sounded crazy. We all knew this from very early on. We figured out this guy was special.

Grocery lists and Data cubes

After coming to campus, I realized that you need a car to get around places. Even if it just means going down to the grocery store. That's the premise of how my association with Venky started.

He had already stayed in the US for five years, a couple of which he had worked for Tandem. He had acquired a car. Our graduate residence was very close to each other, and he was just a few doors down from me. Since he lived just a few turns from me, he used to give me a ride to the grocery store. That's how we got more acquainted with each other. Little did I know that this would be the guy with whom I would start three start-ups.

We ended up picking the same Ph.D. advisor, Professor Jeff Ullman. What solidified our collaboration was the first piece of academic research that we did together. We published a paper on Data Cubes (computer analytic processes) in 1996 and got the Award for the best research paper at the conference. It was called "Implementing Data Cubes efficiently." Ten years down the line, it also was termed the most impactful article to be published in our term. That was an exciting collaboration.

The Yahoos and the Junglees

In September 1993, the first web browser came out around the same time. The first year at Stanford went into browsing. It was such a fascinating subject. So, after the success of our research paper, what Venky and I thought was that we could take some of the research ideas we were working on and implement them on the web. At the time, we worked on database integration by using corporate databases available to us. IBM funded the project. But with the advent of the internet, we thought it would be much more interesting to experiment with data off the internet. But the faculties were not that excited about this prospect; it sounded like a crazy idea. That was also around the same time that Yahoo had started coming up! Being Grad students, just like us, Jerry Yang and David Filo were gaining momentum with this new website. At this point, we could see this big ocean of potential, the internet, waving at us from afar, and we just had to immerse ourselves in it.

That's when we started ideating that if we can't integrate this idea into our research, let's create a company of our own where we could implement our ideas and make something useful out of them. At that time, Venky's girlfriend (now wife) was looking into house listings on the internet through various websites. A task that was proving to be quite a pain. We saw this as the primary use case for database integration and started working on a comparison shopping engine for classified listings on the web. So Venky, his classmate, Ashish Gupta, and I started hacking off at this concept and called it Attercorp (based on the fictional spider that appears in the Lord of the Rings novel series. (Which just went to show how geeky we all were.) It was supposed to be analogous to a web spider trawling the web.

Chahe koi mujhe Junglee kahe

These are lyrics to a song by the artist Mohammed Rafi. It literally translates to "Anyone may call me wild"

So, there we were, on the brink of starting a company. But what do we name it? We had a presentation coming up for a significant investor, and we needed a name that would catch their attention. Attercop was an esoteric name and did not sound very welcoming. We went to Ashish's house to discuss this issue. So, we did what anybody does when a creative block hits them. We whipped out some beers and sat down to talk.

While brainstorming, we came up with an idea. The Bollywood song from the movie Junglee goes like this... *"Yahoo! Chahe Koi Mujhe Junglee kahe..."* Yahoo was a company that a couple of Stanford graduate students had started. And Yahoo! has been a great inspiration for us throughout our journey. So, after Yahoo! comes Junglee! (as per the chronology of the song). And in our state of intoxication, that seemed like we had hit the bull's eyes. After sobering up a bit, though, we came up with a more elaborate justification for the name. You see, the internet is like this massive jungle of information, and people needed someone who knew their way around a jungle; that's where we (the Junglees) come in.

Ashish had worked with IBM and was working in Oracle at the time. Having a lot of industry experience, he took on the task of approaching VCs to raise funding. This was when he fell upon an acquaintance, Rakesh Mathur. Mr. Mathur was a part of numerous start-ups before he came across ours. Ashish convinced him to get on board with us. After seeing the Attercop demo, Rakesh decided to call his mentor, Tsuyoshi Taira or "Taira San", as we came to call him. Taira San got in touch with a group of seven Taiwanese businessmen who were eager to invest in this new "internet thing" but did not have access to it. With the help of Taira San, we managed to raise $50,000 of seed funding. It was time for a change. Ashish made Venky rattle through his Ph.D. and quit his job at Oracle.

Getting out of school

While this was unfolding, Yahoo! had already gained many paces and acquired their first IPO. As the prospect of our own company making it bigger presented itself, I was faced with a tough choice; I would have to drop out of my Ph.D. I approached Jeff about this, expecting a good lecture about what a stupid idea it was. Instead, Jeff surprised me.

He said, "If you think this idea is worth implementing, you should go out there and prove it. If things go south, you can still come back and finish your Ph.D."

That's what made me want to take a leap of faith. It helped me decide that I was excited enough by this endeavor to drop out of Stanford and join my partners.

Do you have chemical?

Many years down the line, I asked Taira San, "What made you believe in us? We were a bunch of students fresh out of college with no business experience before this."

He said, "You have good Chemical."

Actually, what he meant was that we had good chemistry. And his words were very true, as I came to understand. When you start-up, you need to have these heated arguments with your co-founder where the two of you have strikingly different opinions but still be friends after that, whatever the outcome of that argument may be. It's the bad times when the chemistry between you and your partners is tested.

The Washington Post

Our product was focused on the online classified space. We had built an online job listing engine that could integrate job listings from all over the web. But there's only so far you can go with seed funding. So, we started to seek another round of funding. But it turned out that other Silicon Valley investors were not as keen on letting a group of students run a company with their money as Taira San was.

They said to us, "Sure, you have a cool product. But what do you know about running a company?"

I still have some of the rejection letters saved up from those days. Rejection either drives you to quit or forces you to innovate. So, we went with the latter option and started approaching newspapers. With the advent of the internet, all the media publications were scrambling to be the next big online media source. The online classified sector earned good money for them, but there was no exclusive online section for classified. With the use of the internet, there was no limit to the number of ads that could be put up. We went to The Washington Post, one of the major digitally publishing newspapers. They had a great foresight about how the internet would be taking over many aspects of media delivery, including the classified listing. Naturally, newspaper publications would feel threatened by such a disruption. But The Washington Post saw this as an opportunity to invest in our company. They became our first customer for the online listing and invested 5 million to buy a part of our company. Soon, we had massive adoption, and we were hosting classified listings for almost all the US media houses.

Online shopping—the birth of a new normal

The first idea you come up with is hardly the best you can do with start-ups. But the initial days are tough, and you've worked so hard on that one product that you don't feel like letting go of it. But after a point, you just know it's not scaling up the way you want it to. We had our group of customers, but we needed to expand in revenue.

This point in a start-up is when you have to PIVOT. We had a meeting with Yahoo!, and they said since we already have this remarkable technology, why don't we try and apply it to the shopping space. This seemed like a great prospect, and we had wanted to do this for quite a while now. So, after this meeting on Friday, we agreed to meet again on Monday to discuss it further. We worked our asses off that weekend and came up with a comparison shopping engine prototype.

After showing them our demo, Yahoo! became the first customer for our second product. It turned out that shopping was way more interesting from a revenue point of view than job listings in those days (that is still the case). We got a deal with many others after yahoo! And our revenue and usage started taking off. Junglee became very popular during 1997-98. Around that time, Amazon approached us because they were interested in what we were doing and decided to acquire Junglee.

After the acquisition, I went ahead to work for Amazon for another two years as the Director of Technology. I ended up contributing to numerous projects with them, for example, Mechanical Turk.

Aah Ph.D. Here we go again...

So, we did this very successful start-up in the market and eventually got acquired. I figured now was the time to go back and finish my Ph.D. I went back to Stanford and got in touch with Jeff again.

He said, "Sure, you can complete your Ph.D. with us. But now that you've had this company and it has done well, we won't give you an assistantship. You have to pay for your tuition."

And when you're paying for your tuition, you end up finishing the job faster. That's just a Ph.D. 101.

Filling in the gaps

Venky and I got together again and discussed some of the problems we faced while getting Junglee off the ground. We realized that the big-time investors cared more about the financial aspects and not so much about the technical part. They could not appreciate the potential for the disruptive change that technological innovation can bring about. We realized this vast gap in the market, where there were these students who were very enthusiastic about the new technology they had come up with, but did not have the resources to take that technology to the market.

So, we came up with Cambrian Ventures, which worked as a seed fund. Our goal was to identify companies started by students and/or faculty members from universities based on relevant research to provide them with the necessary mentorship and help them raise funding to get their technology to the next stage. We ended up investing in many Silicon Valley companies around the late 1990s and early 2000s. So far, we have funded eleven start-ups, of which two—Transformic and Neoteris have been acquired by Google and Juniper networks respectively.

The Virtuous triangle

A lot of the things I do revolve around these three identities. I fundamentally think of myself as an academic. So, research and teaching are at the core of my experiences. But I also happen to be an entrepreneur who likes to innovate and find ways to bring my innovations to the world. Through these experiences, I gained insights into how the industry functions and can share my insights with the world of emerging technologies powered by people. That's where I can function as an Invest Mentor.

These three aspects form a symbiotic system that can power all fronts of Technological innovation. This system is better explained in terms of The Virtuous Triangle. When an academic, you interact with students with fresh and exciting ideas (much like how we used to be before Junglee). Once you become an entrepreneur, you gain experience, which you can then utilize to mentor other emerging academics with a technology they want to share with the world. As an Invest Mentor, I also come across problems worth solving and research-worthy. All these roles feed one another.

Kosmix turned WalmartLabs

The next stepping stone for Venky and me was founding Kosmix in 2005. It was a social media technology provider. Kosmix powered websites like TweatBeat and Righthealth as well as Kosmix.com to enable users to filter and organize content in social networks.

The fundamental technology we were building at Kosmix is called semantic analysis. Which means to understand the meaning of things. We are applying semantic analysis to social media and trying to understand the connections between people, topics, places, and products.

If you look at the founders and management team of Kosmix, we have significant e-commerce experience, and it was pretty obvious to us that the social genome we were building had serious applications to e-commerce. With the technology of Kosmix, we can utilize information from a person's social media platforms to market to users.

Kosmix expanded its focus from vertical to a horizontal search engine in June 2008, covering all subjects. Then in 2011, Walmart acquired Kosmix and formed it into WalmartLabs, which served as a research division under Walmart. I worked as a Senior Vice President at Walmartlabs for a year before Venky and I decided to move on to the next big thing.

Rocketship.vc

Having built numerous tech-based start-ups from scratch, we wanted to use our knowledge and insights to empower the next generation of tech-based start-ups. We had struck upon another use case for data science and machine learning applications—Venture Capital.

We established Rocketship.vc as a venture capital fund investing in companies using models built through data science. We rely on data from across various industries to make truly informed investment decisions.

The interesting part is that we are the ones who reach out to those companies as opposed to them pitching us ideas. Today, Rocketship.vc invests in start-ups from 14 different countries across the globe, including ones like Apna, Khatabook, Later, and Moglix in India. We plan to keep empowering tech-based initiatives through our funding and industry expertise.

Chapter 8

Building an Ocean

Sarvesh Agrawal

After IITs, I feel Internshala is the most known name among college students. In the past decade, Internshala has built such a strong brand awareness and image. A decade before doing internships became a trend, Sarvesh saw that coming. His sheer focus on making the life of college students easier shows how strong a grasp he has on the interests of students. ISP, Internshala Student Partner, has 10,000 student partners all over India, and it's such a well-managed system while being the biggest student organization in the world.

Small town, big dreams

I hail from a small town in Rajasthan called Nawalgarh. With a population of just 50,000, I was fortunate enough to go to a good school. But it was Hindi medium, and that's the language in which I appeared for JEE. To transition from my small town in Rajasthan to Madras was quite a cultural shock. The second shock wave came to me in the form of a reality check that I had not felt before. From international level chess players to Olympiad toppers, it seemed like my classmates had lived their lives ten folds more than I had. Back home, I was the talk of the town; but here, I was amidst classmates who had achieved so much more, and yet, were so grounded.

More than anything, my experience in IIT was a humbling one. All of us were IITians, and we all had different aspirations. There was no unwarranted sense of superiority. The atmosphere was quite conducive to exploration and innovation.

Angrezi Baaten

As is common in all IITs, English was also the primary instructional language at IITM. And being from a Hindi medium background, this was one of the things I really struggled with. I remember jotting down English words in the Devanagari script in my notebook and later referring to the dictionary or asking my friends about their meanings. Despite my struggles with English, my peers and teachers were very supportive and really encouraged me to get out of my comfort zone. They respected that I was navigating the learning curve. Soon, I started reading some light novels and gradually started watching sitcoms too.

At that time, the GRE was very popular amongst undergraduates. I decided to appear for it as well and ended up ranking first amongst my batchmates! Interestingly, I got 800 on 800 in verbal in English (with 770 in quant). That's when the entire hostel wing gave me a toast, applauding the progress I had made.

I also participated in the institute elections and ended up becoming Hostel Affairs Secretary. Contesting the election and campaigning was a completely different ball game for me. IIT Madras, being highly diversified, posed a unique challenge. I could discern how division existed in society and how it affects people's choices. Even in an IIT, housing some of the brightest minds in the country, people still voted based on language and region. That has just been the political scenario in India for as long as we can remember. I guess some things never change.

In my case, the Civil engineering batch was a very tight-knit group of people, and it was also a very influential group to gain support from. I had also made friends across all the states. So, relatability was not a challenge for me. The fact that I had put in a lot of effort into research and had thought up a comprehensive plan of what I had to do, fetched me a lot of plus points. Biases can only take you so far up the decision-making ladder. Ultimately, people cannot deny the obvious hard work and dedication to the task. That is one of my key takeaways from that experience.

Dhandaa to khoon me hai apne

Coming from a Marwari business background, I was no stranger to running a business. It ran in the blood. My experience, however, was from a more traditional and small-scale grocery shop (*kirane ki dukaan*) that was family-owned, as well as a small factory producing mustard oil. Despite the small scale, the fact that I had been dealing with customers from childhood really shaped the way I think as an adult. My father used to leave the shop in the care of my elder brother and me when he used to go out of the station. The concept of money and its worth, the flexibility of credit (*udhaar*) and the following up on it was first-hand education in customer psychology, and I didn't even know it!

You'd be surprised seeing how many management lessons this taught me. To name a few, handling rejection, display management, product placement, and staying at the top of the competition. India is a country where there are entrepreneurs in every *galli* and *nukkad*. There is so much diversity and so much more to learn. These businesses have been sustaining themselves for generations and generations. They are doing something right.

To be and what to be?

In the final year of my dual degree, most of my friends from B. Tech had passed out, and I found myself kind of alone, left to figure out things for myself. It became evident to me that an entirely new life outside the campus was waiting for me to embrace. I grew very pensive and reflective. This awakened the philosopher in me. And this guy sure had a lot of questions that needed to be answered.

Textbook philosophical questions like, "What is the purpose of my life? What impact have I made on this world? Seven billion people live on this planet, not to mention the quadrillions that came before them. Who remembers them? Most of them are lost to oblivion. Is that the fate I will suffer too? Would it matter to the world that somebody named Sarvesh existed?"

These questions stuck with me for a long time. They played an important role in my path to becoming an entrepreneur. What would I have created that lasts beyond me? It became very central to my thought process and my instinct, and that's what eventually led me to venture out on my own. But first, I needed some industry exposure.

Capital One

I took up a job as a business analyst at Capital One, a UK credit card company. Working in the new product development team, my work involved a lot of customer-centered research and decision-making. We addressed problems like what kind of new products our consumers would like to see, how well-timed our new launch is, etc.

The thing I really loved about Capital One was their sharp focus on work culture. The culture of open feedback and no hierarchy kept things running smoothly. Above all, the culture of keeping customers at the heart of everything we did. I would never have thought I could be happy in a workplace, but I was serendipitously proved wrong. I saw that the moment you get freedom, you are simultaneously motivated. This paired with some room to make mistakes and overcome them right away, really gets you the hang of real-time problem-solving. It's very easy to see how quality work happens at such a place.

In fact, when I was leaving Capital One, I wrote a note to myself that when I start an organization of my own, I'll make sure I'll model its culture based on what I experienced at Capital One.

Capital One was a highly data-driven and analytical space. Every decision was made based on facts and data. Whether you are a CEO or an intern or a senior manager, anyone can question anyone as long as it's based on hard data.

During placements, I had built a notion that computers are just for geeks and that the real work happens in the field. Boy, was I wrong! I justified not learning to code by saying that it would get me a 9 to 5 job and that I wanted to do something on the field and not on a desk. But the fact of the times is that all of us are sitting in front of a computer now.

At Capital One, we were assigned a case study, which took me back to my childhood business experiences. From looking at customer interactions to reviewing costs and pricing, I really enjoyed it and felt very comfortable with the thought of using numbers for making decisions. I realized this was something I was really passionate about and also had an aptitude for.

Then, I shifted to Barclays Bank. It was a multinational bank being set up in India. The experience there was very different from that at Capital One. Let's just say I got exposed to many problems that haunt every large business organization. There were three major lessons that I learned at Barclays.

Firstly, operational rigor. Secondly, how different elements in a business come together to interact and how, sometimes, it produces friction. And thirdly, how *not* to build the culture of an organization. Sometimes, you have to experience the bad to appreciate what is good.

Scholiverse

My last job was at Aviva Life insurance. I finally decided that I wanted to enter the world of entrepreneurship. I did not have a very concrete plan; just a rough notion about the kind of organization I wanted to see turned into reality. I had an idea of a comprehensive learning platform that saw you through your career plans, right from class 8th to all through boards, entrance exams, college, internships, and finally, get you the job you were meant for. It does sound like a long shot in terms of execution. But I think if you want to do something enough, you find a way to make it work. It may take time, and you may have to start off smaller than you envisioned, but there is no upper bound to dreams, right? "Scholiverse" (short for Scholar's Universe) sounded like a good name for this venture.

Back to the ground, my problem statement was very vast and inclusive, and it was evident that I had to look into specifics and dig deeper. I realized a gap in the internship market. There were portals for entrance exam preparation and career counseling, but no place where people could look for internships specifically. This made me look deeper into the fundamental distinctions between a job and an internship and what sort of consumer pool would an internship-specific platform attract.

As luck would have it, I met my batchmate from IIT, who went on to do his MBA at London Business School. He was looking for an internship in India in his first year of summer in MBA. He could not find an internship. Somebody from IIT Madras + LBS not being able to find a good internship in India. Imagine that! Such was the plight of thousands of students from all across the country.

That convinced me that the first challenge we should tackle is the internship. As a first-time entrepreneur, you are naive. At that time, I thought we would solve the internship problem in one year. Then, we would go on building the rest of the elements of *Scholiverse* at the same pace (one every year). Ten years later, we are still working on the internship problem and solving newer challenges every day.

That is how Internshala started to take form. IIT Madras played an important role in making it possible. I think everything goes back to IIT Madras in some way or the other. I learned a lot about relationship building there as a secretary. I learned that you have to work with different people—wardens, Deans, directors, mess workers, engineering unit guys, etc.

Coding ille :(

When I started Internshala, I didn't have any programming experience, and I regretted not learning to program while in college. While I was improving my English earlier, I used to write blogs, which built good writing skills for me. I had good analytical skills, which I learned from my job. I had some idea what culture I wanted to build, and I had some experience recruiting fresh graduates in the organizations I worked at. Finally, I had a problem statement in hand. But since I did not know programming, I decided we'll build a portal a bit later and start with a very basic pilot to test the waters.

I started a blog, "Internshala," and I said, "this will be a single place for internships." Now, this is a two-sided platform. You need students, and you need companies. It's a chicken and egg problem. How do you get students when you don't have internships, and how do you get companies when you don't have students? Then, I reached out to somebody who knew how Sanjeev Bikchandani started Naukri.com as he may have faced the same problem. If there is no company, they won't get users, and if there is no user, they won't get a company.

I learned that there were a lot of job listings that were advertised in newspapers as classifieds back then. For example, if a company needed a salesman or someone needed a teacher. Sanjeev took those listings and he put them on his website. That's how he built his initial few 100 listings.

I did the same too. Whenever I found an internship program on the internet, it could be by IIT Madras, IIT Delhi, or other universities or foreign companies, I started writing blogs for them.

This way, I had about 30-40 really interesting opportunities, all of them in one place, which were not available elsewhere. Then, I started reaching out to the training and placement cells of the top 100 colleges, and they were very happy to help because somebody was helping their students find an internship. They shared my email among the students, and the student-side traffic built up.

Once that happened, I reached out to the IIT Madras alumni cell through my faculty members, and they said, "What kind of help do you want?" And honestly, I didn't know what to do. So, they said, "Hey, why don't you send a write-up, and we'll share it among all our alumni?" At that time, they had Mail IDs of 18,000 of them.

I wrote a nice write-up, sharing, "Hey, this is my side hustle (I hadn't left my job by then), and do you have anything which can help? So, let's connect."

Now, something happened, which I didn't expect. The next morning, when I woke up, I got 800 emails saying, "Hey, it's very nice, very exciting." A few of them wrote, "Why don't you write about our start-up? We want a few interns." A few people wrote, "Hey, can you help my son or daughter in getting an internship?"

So, I think that's the starting off when I realized the size of the problem and that something big was happening. We got about 40 to 50 organic listings from there.

This was the point when I realized, now it's time to go full-time. At the same time, this mail reached someone at IBM, who was also an IIT Madras alumnus. He told me, "We are running a student program at IBM. You share about us and we'll pay you." Well, for an entrepreneur, getting first income is a big experience.

Now, the summer passed, and the traffic of the site started dropping because once the summer is over, internships are done. We were like, "Why would people visit our site now?" Then, we started thinking about what we could do to maintain the traffic. So, we started something called My Internship Story. In this contest, everyone who had completed an internship could share their experience of how it was and what they did in it. This way, we would get a lot of user-generated content, SEO (Search Engine Optimization) would get better, and if someone's story got 100 likes, we would give them 100 rupees recharge as the prize.

Later, we wanted to increase the prize money. And that's when we reached out to IBM again and told them that we were planning such an event and we would like them to sponsor it. They asked for the budget, and I started explaining, the prize money would be 30,000, we would spend 5,000 on marketing. They said ok. That's when I realized I had massively under-sold it. For IBM, 35K was nothing. It doesn't even appear in their balance sheet. But a good relationship with IBM was built, and they started paying 50,000 to Internshala every month to share about their program.

We realized companies like IBM could be good customers while advertising could be a good model on which we could rely.

For the first two years, we relied on advertising entirely. We used to look for the college fest pages and the companies that were sponsoring them. We started reaching out to them. We pitched them to reach out to the college community. Maybe, we can help you put your banner on our site or can add it in the mail to the subscribers. That's when I read the book 'The Google Story,' where they said if you are creating value, monetization will be figured out over time. So, focus on creating value. Somehow, you'll find a way to make money out of it.

The revenue from advertisements continued to grow. The first year, it was six lakhs. The next year, it went to 12 lakhs and then 1.5 crores.

But then, we realized this is not a scalable model. Beyond a point, you can't scale advertising, especially as most advertising was shifting to Facebook or Google. There was a lot of chasing of clients, and then, it will take two months to six months to even get paid. They'll say, it's going to HR, or it's with the finance. I realized this was not my cup of tea. I just hated that. If I had delivered a service to you, my job would have been done. Now, it's your turn to pay.

I realized in India that B2B is very hard and getting money from the customer is even harder.

At the same time, we were seeing one more thing. That is, in 2013-14, there were a lot of students who were applying for internships but not getting selected. Then they would go to the centres of IBM and HP. They used to run small training centres in cities, where these people will pay some 10,000 rupees to learn Java, Dotnet, etc. I realized there were flaws with this model. One is, they were franchising models, so you can't maintain the quality. The second is that they were very expensive. Third, it was not totally accessible by most of the people. If you are from a city like Nawalgarh, it's very tough to go to a city like Delhi to do it.

Then, we said, "Let's build an online training centre." We named it Virtual Training Centre.

So, I didn't know coding again, and IIT played the supporting role. I needed somebody to set up the platform for us and had an email sent to recent alumni of IITM via alumni cell. And Vikram Shah (Class of 2012, Dual Degree, Engineering Design) reached out. He was experienced in building a similar start-up called Lema Labs during his college days at IITM.

He told me that he would build this training platform. Now, we were discussing which course to start with. Vikram said, "Let's make it on web development because I am learning web development for building the platform." We both didn't know how to do programming.

We made a page live, announcing Internshala is bringing the Virtual Training Centre at the cost of 2500 rupees. It was a six-week program, where you would get text tutorials, projects, and our assistance. We would even answer your doubts, etc. We were doing all this when we ourselves didn't have our own website. We were learning web development ourselves. Even though the course wasn't ready, we just put up the page. My idea behind it was if we put so much effort and nobody signs up, it won't be worth the time. It's better that we make something up. We set up a signup page, and we said let's sit back and see how many people apply. We were highly skeptical about it.

We thought students would not spend on it. Why would they pay for such a course when so much is available on the internet? Now, to our surprise, three people bought the course that day itself, which came as a big surprise to us and we were wondering, 'Why are the students paying?' We are neither development experts, nor are we a big firm. We are just still a blog.

When we spoke to those students, we realized that the main asset we had built was the Internshala brand, the cultural values that we talked about, and how it can fundamentally change the brand's trajectory.

I talked about how Capital One taught me to do the right thing, and I said this is the kind of culture I want to build it in.

So, right from day one, we started with this at Internshala.

Internships are a demand and supply market, where companies are the demand and students are the supply side. It's a market very skewed towards the company side. Companies could get away with anything in the name of internships. You could just charge money to students in the name of an internship, and above that, 90% of the internships were unpaid. You actually get paid internships only on campuses like IITs and IIMs.

So, it was just exploitation. We said, "We don't think it is fair for a company to get work out of students and not pay them." From day one, we stood for supply in a market that is so heavily skewed in favor of demand.

Not because of business reasons, but we said that this is not fair and it's just not the right thing to do—to get somebody to work for you and not pay them. You're hiring interns because you expect some work out of them to help your business. Why should this person not be paid?

Right from day one, we were very particular that we would publish only paying meaningful internships, and we always paid attention to our student complaints.

So, back in 2013, when the internet wasn't a big thing, people still went to banks and paid directly to our accounts. That's when we realized this was a scalable business.

Now, two things happened simultaneously: advertising revenue was becoming a plateau, and this online course was building up.

For about three to four years between 2013-2016, we stuck with both of them—online training and advertising. But after 2016, we took a call that advertising is a big distraction and a lot of chasing around. We had to try to achieve a client who could give us a sizable ad deal, and then, run behind him for payment.

We would rather not do any of it and focus on our own product, which was truly a good decision.

I think one thing is that despite tasting early success in online training, we didn't scale it as aggressively as we are doing it right now. I think we lost two years in that period when we were distracted by advertising.

At that time, we realized that both were equally big. Now, we built online training as a sole revenue stream for Internshala. I think a common misconception that students don't pay is not true. I think it is that they need to have a high bar of trust, and they need to really believe that this platform stands for this community.

When people, the faculty members, their friends, and their seniors tell them that Internshala is good and it can help you, students really believe it.

Future of Internshala

Fundamentally, what I think is that we are trying to reach out to 30 million college students in India currently, who we see graduating without enough practical exposure, while focusing on helping them figure out what they really want with their lives and not just with their skills.

If all of us can figure out while we are in college that "this is what I want to do," then you can build a solid portfolio and skill in that domain in four years. Then, our career trajectory is going to be very different. Many of us end up in jobs that we don't like, and then, we sort of cheat on them. You'll see bumpy roads, loose chairs, or an electrician who is trying to fit a wrong screw. I think it all happens when we are stuck with jobs that we don't really enjoy, and all of that gets solved if we could figure out what we really want to do and had experience, exposure, and opportunity. My life, my family's life, and my country's future would all be better off with so much more innovation, creativity, and growth. If all of us could really find our calling! This is a principle with which Internshala operates and enables every college student to find their destiny.

One metric by which we measure ourselves is the number of students who were selected in an internship using Internshala in one year, and that's our *aha* moment. It's not the amount of money we make, no matter how many students come to our platform. Real happiness is when they actually get an internship. That right now is half a million every year. We want to take it to 10 million students over the next few years.

We want to be able to say that every year, 10 million students find an internship or job via Internshala. I think that's one goal that we want to achieve.

The second goal is we did a fabulous job in building the brand. We need to do an equally aggressive job to build up business out of it. One of the immediate goals that we have is that we currently generate about twenty-five crores of revenue. How can we take it to 200 crores in the next two to three years?

Our business and revenue should be commensurate with the brand that we have. The third goal is for Internshala to have a scalable transformation, where we identify different career needs and build a single-stop destination that is kind of already happening.

We aspire to get integrated into India's destiny so deeply that it becomes hard to imagine a student's career without Internshala. Whatever be the future of India we build, Internshala should have a specific role in that.

Brief Chronicles 2

Ravi Saraogi,
Co-Founder and President APAC, Uniphore

When my co-founder Umesh Sachdev and I studied at Jaypee Institute of Information Technology, we were focused and convinced about becoming entrepreneurs and building a deep tech product company. We co-founded Singularis, which was in the mobile technology space. However, we had to rethink the concept due to market constraints. Hence, we were directed to Professor Ashok Jhunjhunwala from IIT Madras, who actively counseled entrepreneurs in the initial stages of their journey. Professor Jhunjhunwala invited us to join IITM's Rural Technology and Business Incubator.

It is noteworthy to say that IIT Madras is a very progressive institute that democratizes access to its resources. One does not have to study at the institute to benefit from its facilities and knowledge base. The institute offers corporates and start-ups the possibility of setting up technical research labs on its premises to further technology innovation and build cutting-edge solutions.

What IIT Madras does is inspirational and dramatically impacts the start-up sector, which has a collaborative ecosystem to grow. The institute was highly forthcoming with knowledge and support from professors (including Prof. Bhaskar Ramamuthi, Prof. Timothy A. Gonsalves – Ex IITM), funding, and interns who helped us innovate while learning during our incubation.

IIT Madras is genuinely leading the way of "Made in India, built for the world."

Chapter 9

The Monk Who Drives a Tesla

Swaroop "Kittu" Kolluri: Founder Neotribe Ventures

Kittu is the most spirited quinquagenarian (a person above 50 years of age) that you are ever likely to come across. For 36 years of his professional career, he has been surfing the waves of software development, management, and for the better part of it, entrepreneurship and venture capital.

As a boy, he played badminton at the state level while singing alongside his mother, a Bharata Natyam and Kuchipudi guru. But all of that ceased when he started to prepare for his JEE Exams. After getting into IITM, he rediscovered himself through the vibrant student culture and emerged as a beloved leader. (Read on to know more about his notions about what makes a good leader.)

Kittu's professional trajectory is an excellent example of how a person can learn and adapt to all stages of their lives. Interacting with him, one is instantly energized. He has a way of putting people at ease, which is why he is such a great mentor for young entrepreneurs.

His insight into the professional world has enabled him to become an informed and invigorated investor. His firm, Neotribe Ventures, is a next-generation-yet-old-fashioned venture capital firm. They invest in people, technologies, and ideas that can be disruptive and transformational! Just as tribes represent small, protective, and caring groups, they believe that start-ups with innovative and aspirational individuals and teams can thrive if provided the security and backing to be unafraid in pursuing new ideas, excellence, and success.

Brace yourself for enlightening epiphanies as he recalls his journey for us.

Before college, I had a life.

I grew up in Hyderabad. When I was in school, I used to play badminton a lot—I even played at the state sub-junior level. Since my mom was a renowned dance guru, I learned Carnatic music. But my father was a pretty strict person, and he really held academic achievement on a pedestal. He shut it all off and pushed me to study for JEE. So, that was that.

Life at IIT

I was allotted Godav (Godavari hostel) to stay for the next four years. During that time, I heard how people were given weird nicknames (some can't even be shared outside college). My grandmother used to call me Kittu. I proposed it and my seniors approved. Since there were so many IITM people in Silicon Valley, it became a common nickname for me here too.

When I came to IIT, I had the time of my life with my newly acquired freedom!

My dad could no longer enforce rules on me. So, I just took all the liberties that I could. I participated in a lot of sports and cultural activities. I represented IIT in cricket at Inter-IIT and music in many college festivals like Festember (NIT Trichy's cultural fest) and Mood Indigo (IIT Bombay's cultural fest). At IIT, I finally got to explore to my heart's content. My academics did take a back seat due to that, but so be it. I believe that in all technical institutes, your left brain gets exercised too much, and your right brain is left pretty much unattended. The extracurriculars that I was involved in helped me exercise my right brain more.

I was never a morning person. So, the 8 a.m. class used to be a real pain! I used to wake up at the last moment and barely make it to breakfast, miss the first class, and then make it to the next one.

After a series of classes, we used to have these workshops in the afternoon, being Mechanical engineering students. In hindsight, they were pretty enjoyable as we got to do things hands-on. But at that time, there was a guy called Goodman who was the shop's foreman. Oh, the man was a SADIST! That was something all of us could agree on at the time. Let's just say he made it very difficult for us to enjoy the workshop.

Despite these rants, college life, in a nutshell, was a very liberating experience for me.

Postion Of Responsibilities in College

In my second year, I became the General Secretary of the hostel. Then, I stood for the institute's General Secretary but lost by a small margin. Although I was pretty active and popular on campus, and participating in elections was not political, but I felt strongly about certain things. So, these places gave me a chance to voice my opinions. I just wasn't satisfied with the status quo. Authenticity mattered to me more than anything else. With me, what you see is what you get. That is what made me a successful general secretary for the Godavari hostel.

But being the general secretary taught me a great deal about myself. When we think about intelligence, we all think about our native intelligence. The one thing that we don't think about or learn how to hone is emotional intelligence, and in my experience, it's EQ that is way more important than IQ.

See, your native intelligence will take you to a certain level as a student or when you get into the corporate world as an individual contributor. But you need to learn how to work with others, get stuff done from others, and extract the best out of others. You need self-awareness. The world is not all logical and ideal, and we should be armed to deal with human unpredictability.

I went into IIT as a young nerd who was very good in academics but a dummy in all other (and, in my opinion, more important) aspects. But I came out of IIT with a more well-rounded education. I did not just leave with a degree in Mechanical Engineering. After exploring all my means of self-expression, I could really blossom as an individual with an independent mind. My time here enabled me to become a good leader. My managers recognized that in me, so I was quickly promoted after starting my job in Silicon Graphics.

The Three Leaders

There are three levels of leadership that you are likely to encounter across all workplaces.

The first level is what I call Effective Leadership. Effective leaders focus on personal excellence. They want to get the best out of themselves, and they really put themselves out to prove their effectiveness. Whether you are a student or an individual contributor, you're trying to be the best you can be. And sometimes, that comes at the expense of others because it becomes a zero-sum game when you are competing. After a point, you realize that personal excellence can only take you so far.

The next level is what I call Inspired Leadership. Inspired leaders are the ones that realize that I can't just focus on personal excellence. I need to get to interpersonal excellence. It's all about how I work with others, for others, and to get others to work for me. Together with them, I can achieve something that no one person can. People ARE essential, but people are a means to an end, which is still YOU.

The third type of leadership is what I call Beloved Leadership. Beloved leadership is when people are the end! You get joy from seeing others succeed. This is not something kids will understand at the first mention because you have to overcome many insecurities as you evolve in your personal and professional lives. But please remember, that's the goal, where whatever you do for someone else is the purest form of selfishness. You will come to realize that it is the greatest self-service.

I wish I had been more Disciplined

Once I got my freedom in IITM, my pendulum swung the other way, and I ended up neglecting my academics to some extent. There was a much better way I could have handled that newfound freedom. That was a place where I felt that I never unlocked my full academic potential. I really thought at the time that my slack in academics would harm me in the long run.

I ended up not doing so because once I went to grad school, I made the pendulum swing back in a big way. So, I did very well in grad school and focused on academics. I did well in my work life because I got serious about it. So, commitment to excellence is fundamental.

Shifting towards Silicon Graphics

I graduated in 1986 and was selected at the University of Buffalo. Since there were five months until I went there, I had some time to kill. So, my friend and I watched movies every day. Sometimes, even two in a day. My father found out about it and scolded me.

He said, "Why are you wasting your time? Why don't you go look for a job, work for at least a few months before you leave?"

So, I went and interviewed at a couple of places. One of them was an Indo-Czechoslovakia joint venture called Praga Tools. Since I was a mechanical engineer, I got a job offer. But then somebody told me about this company called OMC computers in Secunderabad.

So, on a whim, I walked in and said, "I'm a recent graduate of IIT. Do you guys have any job?"

"Okay, we'll test you."

They asked me to go into the lunchroom and gave me the test paper. I aced it. I was asked to sit down while she corrected the paper. Then, a few minutes later, the director of software engineering came up and said, "You can do very well in this. We'd like to hire you."

I went to my dad and said, "Okay, you asked me to get a job. Now, I have two jobs. And I think I'm going to go join OMC computers."

He said, "Are you stupid? You should join Praga tools." (They are under the Defense Ministry now). That is like the Government of India's job.

I said, "Dad, I am not staying here, and I am going for a Master's. What's the point in joining? At least, at OMC, I'll learn some new skills."

Honestly, it was a huge inflection point in my life. Your life, too, will have lots of inflection points. Some of them will be by design, and some will be by accident. In this case, conventional wisdom would be joining Praga tools, but I went with OMC, which changed my life. Because that is what pivoted me from mechanical engineering to computer science.

When we join an IIT, we don't really know whether our aptitude is for mechanical or civil engineering. First of all, it's not even clear that you have a freaking passion for engineering, let alone have any notion about your branch. You get into IIT because you did well in JEE. When I was a senior, I was interacting with this junior of mine. His AIR was 747, and he took Aero (Aerospace Engineering). I asked him why he took this branch.

He said, "Sir, I want to become a pilot!"

I looked at him and said, "You don't become a pilot with Aero engineering, you idiot!"

When you enter IIT, you don't know what your passion is. When you are 18–19 years old, and someone is telling you to follow your passion, they are bullshitting you. Those select few have the conviction to follow through with their resolutions, but most of us were clueless. After getting into IIT, you get a much clearer picture of what things are and could be.

In fact, that job at OMC helped me do that. I loved being a software engineer. When programming, you enter a zone, and I loved being in that zone. Listen to Kishore Kumar or Lata Mangeshkar songs with everything quiet and your headphones on. That's when I discovered I loved it.

Working at Silicon Graphics

I joined Silicon graphics in 1990. I was married by then. I used to go to the office around 9:30-10 a.m., which was kind of late. But that's because we used to be awake until about 1 a.m. during the night.

In a couple of years, people, including my managers, recognized my leadership skills, and they quickly promoted me to engineering manager. I was the youngest engineering manager, and that's because they saw that leadership potential. I'd say that was because I could attract others to come to join me. People saw that I was doing a good job, but I was able to work well with others and inspire them to go above and beyond the call of duty.

That's how the days went by, and by late 1995, I had established myself well in the company. The founder of Silicon Graphics, Jim Clark, actually knew me and my work well.

In 1992, Jim started a company called Netscape and asked me to come to join him. I turned him down (for reasons that seemed valid at the time). I was working on an interactive television project that I thought would change the world. I was underwhelmed by Netscape.

BOY, was I wrong! Fortunately for me, Jim came back in late 1995 to recruit me to join him at Healtheon. The Healtheon journey was exhilarating! We took the company public in early 1999! I stayed on till the end of 2000, before leaving for Neoteris.

Neoteris

Then, I advised a few companies. One of them was this company called Dana Street. I helped the founders pivot from a B2C business model to a B2B business.

They came to me upfront and said, *"Hey, you're as much part of this new incarnation. Why don't you come to join us?"* So, that's how I joined them and took over as CEO. Later on, we renamed Dana Street Neoteris. That was my second start-up. I helped attract investment from Jim Clark.

NEA & Neotribe Ventures

I am 56 and have considerable experience in investing. So, at this stage, I am most useful to young entrepreneurs. If I just focus on one company, I don't have as much impact. I view venture capital as a means to an end. I get to help multiple companies instead of being selfish and doing one company. The companies I invest in get more of me than just capital. Capital is easy; many people out there can offer you that. But what young entrepreneurs need is company-building experience. That is what I bring to the table. I can provide them with the expertise and guidance they may need to make their business work. And it's a win-win situation; if they prosper, I prosper.

After Neoteris got acquired by Juniper Networks, I spent a couple of years at Juniper as EVP and General Manager of the Enterprise business. I then joined the venture capital industry as a General Partner at New Enterprise Associates (NEA). NEA is a huge firm. We were investing out of multi-billion-dollar funds. But the problem was that as the size of the fund grows, generating attractive returns on it becomes harder and harder. I felt like there was a better way of doing this. That is how Neotribe came into being. We found that investing smaller funds aligned with me as an investor and with my limited partners.

When I started Neotribe, I started off as a solo GP (General Partner), and it was probably the most challenging thing that I have ever done. Until my first closing, I could not get anyone to join me as partners, apart from our CFO. Limited Partners don't usually invest in single GP firms.

There are a million questions they ask you, like "How much of the success of this firm is actually a part of NEA?"

I got my other partners to join me much later on.

For me, generating deal flow (start-ups looking for capital investments in companies) wasn't an issue. Over the past 32 years here in Silicon Valley, I am fortunate to have built a body of work, a lot of goodwill, and a personal brand. A lot of people know me just by my nickname, Kittu. Even when I was doing Neoteris, I started to make angel investments in companies that came to me for advice. I was a small-scale seed investor before I became a VC. After I joined NEA as a general partner, there was some publicity for my journey to NEA. And the immigrant community, particularly the IIT community, here is huge. So, generating deal flow was not difficult; it was just choosing a company.

In all businesses, you make false positives and false negatives. But one thing about early-stage venture capital is that false negatives are more expensive than false positives. But at Neotribe, our scale is still comparatively small. We are unlikely to have more than five partners in the firms, and here, I get to do something that can actually make a difference in these businesses —something more valuable than the money, a vision of the future.

What The FISH?

In my professional career of nearly 35 years, I sometimes have, by design, sometimes by accident, alternated between being a small fish in a big pond and being a big fish in a small pond.

When I worked at Silicon Graphics for six years, I was a small fish in a big pond with so many employees; I was just one of them.

At Healtheon, I started off as a big fish in a small pond, where I was in the top three people of the company. It became public, and I became a small fish in a much bigger pond.

When I joined NEA, I was one of the general partners, but it was a large firm of 65 people. So, I was a small fish in a large pond. When I started Neotribe, I was a big fish in a small pond.

You get to learn different things by doing this. When you are a big fish in a small pond, you have to do everything yourself. So, you get cross-functional experience. But when you are a small fish in a big pond, you learn one thing really well and at scale.

Now, I prefer being a big fish in a small pond because you can impact more things, particularly in my industry (venture capital). You can't scale. Where you can take a $200Mn fund, you can 2-4x it, but you can't do the same on a repeatable basis with a $2Bn fund.

Chapter 10

The 100-Hour Work Week

Detect Technologies: Daniel Raj David, Harikrishnan AS, Karthik R, Tarun Kumar Mishra

We interviewed Daniel Raj David, who walked us through the whole journey of how Detect came to be. Daniel's narrative helped us envision the dynamics of the victorious collaboration among the company founders. Each of them played to their strengths to make Detect Technology the company that it is today.

This chapter makes you appreciate the importance of connections that you form early on in your life and how you can make things work with collaboration and communication.

In many stories and most movies, you see just one protagonist. But in the case of Detect, the stories of four people are so serendipitously interwoven that it comes together as a single, awe-inspiring narrative. There are several pieces to the puzzle.

As Daniel helps us bring this puzzle together of how Detect came to be...

Getting placed at Jamshedpur

This story started far before I came into the picture. Tarun Mishra, an IIT Madras grad, 2008 batch metallurgy, was researching under Professor Krishnan about Non-Destructive evaluation. It is basically the technology to assess a structure or identify a structure's health without damaging its integrity.

By 2013, his graduating year, they had filed a patent (which was granted both in India and the United States) for **the first sensor in the world that can generate Ultrasonic signals at higher temperatures** (close to around 350 degrees Celsius). All of this was pure research and they were far from finding a use case for this newly acquired technological arsenal.

Tarun got an award for being in the top 10 innovators in India as part of the Innovation Growth Program. He was the only student among the 10. Everyone else was either a prior entrepreneur, professor, or a research expert. He came back to IITM for the placement rounds and then, through some divine intervention, he got placed at Reliance Jamnagar. Which was and still is the world's largest refinery; the refinery itself is the size of your entire city of Central Mumbai. Imagine a city filled with assets like stacks, boilers, pipelines, and all kinds of various large machine installations.

This was where it all started

Tarun accumulated considerable expertise while coming into this industry. He was the Imposter!

He was there to learn all their ways and managed to learn all their tasks, in the hope that once he was ejected (leaves the company), he would pilot a spaceship of his own (run his own company). He was not there to make a career out of it. He just wanted to see where the gaps were so that he can make his enterprise more foolproof.

He was much like Flipkart's founder who had been working for Amazon for a long time. He excelled at his job and spent the rest of the time prying about the departments that he had nothing to do with, just to see what their issues were.

Daniel's Narrative at IITM

I got into the campus in 2012. Like most of the students during my second year, I was just mailing professors right and left to see if there was any work. Incidentally, I ended up speaking to Professor Krishnan as well and I was given the responsibility of building on top of Tarun's technology. I looped in my best friend cum roommate, Hari (Harikrishnan AS). He was also the branch topper for mechanical engineering in our batch. We ended up finding a handful of people, who wanted to work on technology that could see the light of day at some point in the industry. Now, the turn of events was such that Tarun had gained a lot of experience by then, working at Reliance. He came back to the drawing board, but now, with a problem statement.

The beauty of being a second-year student is that you are not intelligent enough to know that something might not work. I think that is the driving factor for innovation to a vast extent. The second factor was exposure. Tarun was the bridge between us and the industry. Because as a second-year student, you do not get that much info; you get that exposure only when you leave campus. But when you leave campus, you are not sheltered anymore; the stakes are much higher, you have far more responsibilities and you don't have the ecosystem to play around with.

I think what we realized early on was that this was an opportunity to make a difference. Although starting up was not on my mind, I think it was on Tarun's. For Hari and me, it was incentive enough that we were working on something that is going to save lives. Secondly, it was cutting-edge research. It's not like working on this came at the cost of our academic futures. We were learning, building on something which was a patented technology. It is something that did not exist anywhere in the world. So, any incremental work you do on top of that would be beneficial to the overall society. So, morally, emotionally, and from a future financial perspective, it ticked all the boxes, while we had nothing to lose. The only way was forward.

People were running behind Positions of Responsibility (POR). I didn't bother too much about it. I thought that if you're building something worthwhile, you will automatically get into a position of responsibility because you're making something valuable.

On campus, you see a lot of races going on simultaneously. There are people running for PORs and leadership roles. A considerable fraction of students put in a lot of effort to gain those things. The other fight was on the Academic side, where these things were kept on the sidelines and the dealing was on the GPA. These two races were always in motion and the top spots were always in demand. But I wanted to do something different from what I was surrounded by.

The work we were doing allowed us to kind of transcend all of these rat races that were going on and get a taste of the real world for ourselves.

All this sounds very philosophical at the surface level. But it turns out to be visionary once it starts to work out well. Hari and I both had it in us to withstand that risk of taking the unconventional path.

The Problem

The power plant industry has something called shutdowns that happen on a site every year, and these shutdowns can last for about 40 days. Each day, the production loss of the shutdown is about a couple of million dollars. In fact, the shutdown scheduled for sites shouldn't be known publicly because it is known to affect share markets. These measures are necessary because your equipment cannot last forever. They have to shut down production to inspect the equipment, carry out maintenance procedures and replace certain parts if necessary. Imagine this being done at the scale and magnitude of a city like Mumbai (like in Reliance Jamnagar). This was a major setback that the industry had to deal with due to the nature of their operations.

This is a problem that is seen across the standards and all across the world. In 2019, the whole Philadelphia refinery in the US had to completely shut down permanently because of a pipeline explosion. Also, maintenance activities happen in dangerous environments; you have loads of safety protocols for the maintenance workers. If a safety protocol is not followed stringently or adequately, there is a chance of an incident happening and people dying. Like in the US construction space alone, about 900 people die every year just by not following three fundamental basic safety necessities: your helmets, your harnesses, and the right practices for work at height. So, safety is a big issue and a big concern.

Furthermore, note that most of the critical pipes in these sites are operating at temperatures anywhere between 200-400 degrees Celsius. So, there is no way to actually monitor these facilities or monitor these pipelines in real-time.

In fact, if you take an enormous asset like a stack or a boiler or furnace, these are assets that are anywhere between 60 meters to all the way to 250 meters in height. And just to give you a comparison, a three-story building is about 10 to 15 meters in height. So, you can understand the size and the scale at which we are working.

Funding

So, we had this technology that could enable us to build ultrasonic sensors that would operate at higher temperature ranges. Now, how do we take it to the industry? We started discussions with Reliance, a big promoter of novel technologies in India. They collaborated with IIT Madras and invested in building this technology forward.

They came in and said, "We'll give you $100,000 to buy whatever is needed as capital expenditure to use the resources. Then, we'll see where it goes from there. However, if any commercial technology comes out of this, we should get some benefits out of it." That was the deal structure signed between IIT and Reliance, and a meeting went all the way to several higher officials in the Reliance ecosystem. Big gears had been set into motion and we were just a part of a much bigger machine.

Building technology

After this deal, things really started kicking off. IIT Madras had not known many startups in this space; Aether was just coming up at that time. Hyperverge was doing a completely different business line then and they were also relatively new. But no one had really integrated various other technologies together, and this was not a mechanical engineering problem alone. We needed software, signal processing, and AI to do that. The requirements of mechanical engineers, metallurgical engineers, electrical engineers, etc., arose.

We needed a much larger spectrum of inputs and we clearly didn't have a team large enough or sophisticated enough to do that. I think that's when we could see all the work that was cut out for us. We needed to assemble a team of people who could be leaders in the future, are great at their particular research areas, and have a thirst to create something that would directly save lives.

CFI enters the battlefield

CFI was the hub for everything then. This was before we had Karthik on the team. We approached them and said, "We need to build out these electronics modules and multiple other modules, both on various sides and we don't have the right team. We don't have a large group; it's just three or four of us and it's too much work to do."

We needed to build a diverse, integrated, and large group, the likes of which were never assembled before at the college level.

What we got in reply was, "Sure, we will help you put this thing together. But the IP (intellectual property) rights should go to CFI and not to you guys."

In their defense, they brought up a lot of draconian terms. I thought that it was a very ballsy move for a student organization to make. But after all, we too were students and did not hold much leverage.

What we ended up doing was we brought in Karthik who had grown past the whole CFI phase at that time and was already placed. We started poaching CFI students for lack of a better term. We were identifying outstanding students or the best in their specific fields of work and not just academically. Some people had put in physical work to ensure that their theories work out; we started pulling them in. I think that momentum, to a large extent, also helped when we did mass hiring. These were close to 40-45 students from campus. They were paid very little. They either worked for the experience or they were being paid 5 to 10K per month. So, money was in no way compensating for the amount of cognition and hard work that they put in; it was more about them buying into the principles and the vision with which we were starting this project.

For instance, Karthik had his Goldman Sachs offer, but was just so enthusiastic about a client saying, "This is wonderful and will save so many lives all because of you." A couple of days later, Karthik told us he was letting go of his Goldman Sachs offer and that he wanted to build this with us. That motive, the need to create a change, was something common across the founding team and all the people we recruited. During our placement season, we found ourselves actually taking the interviews!

Trying to pitch in Mumbai

We never started out with the intent of starting up. We just wanted to make a change with our work. It turned out that starting up was the best way to do it. We realized organically that you need a whole lot of people working together to bring about actual change.

We decided that we can't be dependent on just one client or one customer. The next step was to start contacting organizations like BPCL, HPCL, and the rest of the industry. This was critical because we needed to build a clientele to build revenue.

Today, many business books would tell you never to put all your eggs into one basket (in this case, a client), even if investing in that client would give you a large source of revenue. Because it is entirely dependent on the cycles that that client would follow. But we failed in our attempts to diversify the risks. It was a tad bit comical when we used to meet with potential clients because we were a bunch of kids in our twenties and everyone looked super young. We used to schedule the meeting through our professor or through other contacts.

We were looking to access other facilities and we ended up taking a train to Mumbai to make a presentation. The first question that we were asked was how old we were. The answer was, I think, 20 or 21, and I realized that that was the wrong move for the whole length of the presentation. Despite it being super cool technology, not a single person listened. They just shut off.

Working around the age gap

We came back dejected, but sat down and started thinking. Why were these meetings so severe? Was it just our age or were we not presenting the right things at the right time? That's when we started taking on mentorship. We started working with the IITM incubation cell. Although we hadn't incorporated the company, they were already building a mentoring ecosystem. In fact, we had met people like Gopal Sir (Gopal was the previous MD of Sunmarg Chemplast, and an IITM alumnus) and he has quite a bit of experience running that organization. If you're doing anything industry-related from Chennai, you won't get many people with more experience than him.

He was really invested in the team and the technology and wanted the entrepreneurs to succeed. Those are the people you want to bring in. I think we hit gold there; we had our mentor, framed our presentations better, and started putting ourselves out there. We started going to the student competitions and we had won all the student competitions that existed by this point in time.

Then I realized that the age question never left; it kept coming up in every meeting. So, my mission before every session was to ensure that each question comes at the end of the meeting, because at least then, people listen to the whole presentation before making judgments. That's where the mentorship really helped. I always cracked a joke in my interviews whenever this question came up. I grew a beard purely so that the problem could be avoided and I was quite thankful for my genes that this happened.

I think we put a lot of scrutiny into what a young person can do. Ritesh Agarwal (CEO of OYO rooms) did far more than I have ever done when he was younger than me. In fact, in India, you see a lot of young people taking matters into their own hands. That's where the X factor comes in. The X factor is the fact that we don't know if something can be done and I think that's the beauty of being young that should never be taken away.

What we experienced was a symptom of a problem with the industry. It was a little disheartening because, in my third year's summer, Hari and I had ended up interning at Michigan. In the US, we saw the collaboration between industries and universities, the way they fund facilities, and how they are ready to provide prospective vendors. If someone provides a solution, the industry welcomes them with open arms.

When we returned to India, we noticed that IITM was trying the same. It was one of the few universities in the ecosystem. But it was still fresh. We saw the same potential in this industry and that's why it was a no-brainer. But the challenges that we faced really got us wondering. This is why technology is built abroad and that's why Indian facilities are left with no choice but to import technologies.

Still, if you're importing technologies from somebody else's use case, you might have a slightly different purpose. You have to localize technology-building; you can't depend on what a Shell wants if you're a BPCL. We came back in the summer of 2015 with these radical thoughts that we need to build this ecosystem in India, like we need to invest here because we have the talent and the research capabilities. All we need is a leap of faith. We need to bridge the gap between industries and universities.

Two factors were a great help to us. One was the government. You had the Startup India initiative that started a while back, right when the BJP government came into play. The second big thing was that the IITM Research Park was being built and with efforts from Professor Ashok Jhunjhunwala, Professor Krishnan, and the Director, we're all trying to push forward and work against the challenges together.

The Rookie and his Audacity

In my fourth year, India's oil and gas ecosystem decided to set up 100 crore funds to just provide to startups. OCC (Overseas Construction Company) has their own, probably 50 crores that they can invest. There was this colossal opening ceremony where they publicized this. They brought in a few startups trying to make a change to have a panel discussion with the industry leaders—these giants, the Managing Directors of all of the oil and gas PSUs. They would come and sit there and listen to them.

We were invited to contribute, and at this point in time, we were working only with Reliance.

There were seven of us in the panel. I was the youngest and there were a few other people who had been trying to build companies in the oil and gas ecosystem until then. Everyone was just talking about how great it is that the government had taken this initiative to give a couple of crores per startup, possibly to help these startups prosper. I think when the mic came on, I ended up being the opposite of what all of my counterparts were saying.

Again, I think the beauty of being a student is that you don't know that you shouldn't do something. I ended up telling the industry that it is significant that the government has set this up. But if the funds are not provided to us, if we end up in meeting rooms, and if the industry is not open to listening to the change that can be created through technology, then the impact is going to be minimal despite many crores invested into these organizations. Of course, money is good, but that's not good enough.

At the end of the day, revenue dictates everything, not investment. That's been another philosophy that we truly believed in and we've stuck to till date. Many companies think that they need to raise several rounds of funding. The more you raise, the better and more profitable you are, and of course, the market also chases you the moment you're making a market acquisition. But as a company, our philosophy was to be profitable and for profits to come in sooner than later.

We didn't want to acquire a billion-dollar market and *then* figure out how to make this whole business profitable. We wanted it to be a profitable solution from day one. So, you have to really create differentiated products that solve large problems. I went on this whole tangent of you guys having to support us by action and not by money. You have to ensure that you install technologies, test them out and provide your field as a test area.

After saying all this, it dawned on me that I may have rubbed shoulders the wrong way. These were all super-experienced people. They had to listen to a 21-year-old when they had run these businesses for three to four decades. Thankfully, it ended up having a very positive connotation. Of course, many middle-management people were probably offended by what was said, but many people at the top resonated with this thought process.

After that, we have a lot to owe to BPCL. I think a few of the directors of BPCL had sent people to IIT Madras just to meet that boy who spoke so vehemently against the industry, and they came. The reason they came in matters. It was not to go and prove to us that 'hey, we're going to see we're helping you guys out and we want to see what you can do for us.' But it was more from a standpoint that we want to show India's youngsters that we are willing to change. That was the first big win for us.

So, in 2015, there were a few directors from BPCL who came down. Then, a few directors from HPCL joined them and a few people from Reliance. We had slowly started our business development activities as well. That was a big turning point.

This was basically them coming to us saying, "Hey, show us what you have got. We will see what we can do with it. Given that there is bureaucracy involved, we will help you get through it. We have funds separately allocated for this."

We asked them for a couple of things.

We said, "We wanted you to open up sections of the refinery where we can test."

You need several certifications to enter these dangerous environments, and certificates take years, or at least six months. We suddenly saw that industry people were coming to IIT Madras to figure out how they can take the technologies into their industries. That was the change we wanted to bring in.

Raising Funds

When Hari and I were close to graduation, we realized our sales cycles were long. It took six to seven months to convert a deal then. Right now, it's down to one to two months because there's a structure to take care of it. But then, as a student, it really takes a while to manage the process. We needed to raise money. Our investors were still doubtful as to whether Deep Tech is an area to invest in. Aether had grown, but had not released the product yet. So, success was not seen.

But there are always these gems you come across if you put yourself out in the market enough. I remember going to this Thai conference, where there was a competition of a few minutes for the pitch. Some organizations that were there had made a couple of crores of revenue. We were at literally two lakh revenue, nowhere as close. It was 2016. But what we had was ready technology. So, I ended up putting my heart out there. Speaking about the differentiation of the technology, we ended up winning the competition.

That's where I met my first investor. A guy named Ashwin. He came and said, "Your technology sounds interesting. I am running a fund that is supposed to invest in Deep Technology in India and can scale outside of India." That was their mandate.

So, I said, "This is perfect because this is not conventional. We are not conventional as well, and there are not many funds like this that exist; there has to be a reason we met."

We stayed in touch. He used to call me once every two, three weeks just to get updates on how things were going. And there was a large Reliance deal that we were expecting. I ended up meeting Murugappa Sir, who comes to the IITM Research Park a lot. He's the chairman of the Murugappa group. He looked at our technology and said it was worth investing in.

Then, XLR ventures, started by Kris Gopalakrishnan (the co-founder of Infosys), loved the technology as well. So, things were finally catching a lot of momentum. I would say 2016 was an active year of speed. We participated in close to 25 competitions and won each and every one of them. I think we were down to our last pennies. We were just incorporated and we had to recruit a few people. We were down to the last paisa that we had in the accounts and I remember the award for this competition was 30 lakhs. It was the Wharton India startup challenge by Wharton University. The competition also had many startups that were there in the market for years and had made good revenue versus our startup, which was just starting in revenues and had incorporated that year. It was grueling. But at the end of it, we were chosen as number one and the money was back in our account. We could pay our people. Then, we decided that there has to be a reason for this.

We believe in divine intervention at some level as well. We can't let go of this now. I went to the market and understood everything required to raise your round of funding, whether it is your financial sheets, investor decks, or how to position the key things that an investor looks at. I did something of a crash course. I did not attend a single day of college in my fourth year.

The Glow everyone asked for

In 2017, Saif partners came in. They had been hearing a lot about us in the market. BPCL and Shell started speaking about us and the Reliance projects were successful. Slowly, Detect was building a name across the ecosystem. Then, investors heard from Saif partners. I remember he visited IITM Research Park; we had a smaller office then. He came in and I explained the entire model to him. He just sat with me.

He asked me, "What do you want to be? What is it you're doing this for?"

I realized that these are very core questions, because do you want to be a company that eventually builds and gets acquired at a good value? And you exit as a founder. Then, how you create the organization would change. You would solve many short-term problems to build up valuation and then, maintain relationships with strategic parties to come in and buy.

Now, the right answer to an investor is to show them that within five to ten years, you will give them an exit because that's how long their funds would last? That's the right answer.

But the passionate explanation or the real answer that we had in our minds was that we wanted to build a legacy. I really wanted this to be sustainable. Hence, you would build for profitability, stability, and sustainability instead of just gunning for valuation. In India, we are yet to have Indian products that sit in all facilities around the world that are physical. I said that's what we want to be. If we have to give our investors an exit as we'll be a profitable organization, we will make sure that you don't want to exit. So, that was the play there. And they bought in. They invested and they have been great investors. So far, we did a three-and-a-half million dollar round with them.

Their scale now and future

We had even looked at other problem statements. We started building AI for detecting defects in an automated fashion from either drone cameras or regular cameras. We started doing that with thermal imaging as well because our lab had expertise in thermal imaging.

We took up a mission to build the first drone in the world that can contact structures and apply ultrasonic gels the way your doctor uses ultrasonic gels on people. We were thinking, "Why can't drones go apply and then take measurements? Then, can we thoroughly scan at all points of time?" The same safety risks were happening across all sites. So, our next mission and vision were growing bigger through talking. While we had almost no money in the account, a small fund was put in by Reliance into IIT Madras. It's exciting when you have a bunch of the top talent, close to 45-50 people, sitting in a room together, creating and figuring out what is possible—what can we build? Those were some of the most memorable experiences from my student life—at least that's what made us think big.

We ended up investing in a couple of business development folks. Close to 65 enterprise clients from India started working with us. You name any oil and gas player; they are our clients. They spoke to Detect Technology for anything that they wanted to bring into the industry. We ended up having four offices with Chennai as our headquarters. We were also in Mumbai, Delhi, and Singapore.

We get told a lot of times that if we made a change in India, then we can make a change abroad. Because if you make technology low cost enough for the Indian market, it is going to be tremendously low cost for international markets in this space. We raised a couple of rounds of funding; close to $4.5 million. So far, we are present in Singapore, working with clients like Shell and Exxon, the world's most prominent players. We are working all across India. The whole ecosystem is very well aware of what Detect does. In the US, we've started making waves with facilities like Shell, Exxon, Chevron, and an indirect presence through partners in the Middle East. We have a little bit of activity in the UK and Europe as well. But we're investing substantially into India, Southeast Asia, the US, and the Middle East. These are the core markets that we're targeting. And right now, we can invest more and more resources into creating the change that we've made in this country to bring it to the rest of the world.

Chapter 11

The Power of the Internet

Anant Agarwal: Founder and CEO – edX, MIT Professor

"In 2012, I met Anant, and I thought to myself, 'Who is this crazy guy, and what are his ideas?'. Today, after years of working with him, I still think he is crazy but in a very good way," said Johannes Heinlein—Chief Commercial Officer & Senior Vice President of Strategic Partnerships at edX.

It makes one wonder what kind of a boss Anant Agarwal is to invoke such a description. However, all our doubts were dissolved when we spoke to him during the interview for this chapter. His easy manner and ability to instantly connect with people make him a fantastic teacher and sensational entrepreneur. One should not be fooled by his gray hair because his unending enthusiasm and spontaneity far surpass that of any youth.

Agarwal is the Founder and CEO of edX, originally started as a not-for-profit venture by Harvard University and the Massachusetts Institute of Technology (MIT). He focused on transforming online and on-campus learning through groundbreaking methodologies, game-like experiences, and cutting-edge research. His tenure as a Professor of Electrical Engineering and Computer Science at MIT ran for 33 years and is still going strong. He also launched five profit startups with his students during these years.

His vision with edX is based on his firm belief that education is a right and must be accessible to everyone, much like the air we breathe. The whole endeavor at edX is toward bringing high-quality education to the masses for free or at a low cost!

In March 2016, he was awarded the Harold W. McGraw, Jr. Prize in the Education category for his contribution to higher education. He received Padma Shri, the fourth highest civilian award in the Republic of India, in 2017. In 2018, he received the Yidan Prize for Education Research, the world's largest education award worth USD four million. IIT Madras takes great pride in having him as a Distinguished Alumnus.

As the CEO of edX, Anant continues to bring forward innovations in the world of online learning. He is truly making a mark on history. Here is his story.

A wee lad from Mangalore

Though I was born in Lucknow, I lived in Kaprigudda, Mangalore. I started my entrepreneurial journey when I was 12 years old. Our house in Mangalore housed a chicken farm where we had over 40 hens. It was my job to make rounds and sell the eggs laid by the hens to my neighbors. However, it proved to be a fairly inconsistent venture, as my neighbors' consumption was not enough to meet the supply of eggs we had. I first discovered B2B when I started selling those eggs to a restaurant kitchen that used to buy my entire stock. I got a reasonable price for it too.

My father was a doctor and was teaching at the Kasturba Medical College as a professor. My mother was a homemaker, but she had an entrepreneurial streak in her. She established a home business, a shop which we called Agarwal Agencies. My brother Ruchir Agarwal runs that shop now.

I have academics as well as entrepreneurship in my blood. That is why edX answered my calling.

Mangalore to Madras

At that time, IITs were not so well-known among the common men. When I broke the news of my getting admitted to IIT Madras, my relatives were somehow distraught! They had hoped that I would get admission into one of the local institutions.

Coming from a small town did have its own setbacks. I had never encountered calculus-based physics throughout my education in Mangalore up to the 12th standard. Once I was in IIT Madras, every Physics course I signed up for showed me how glaringly ill-prepared I was for the rigors of university. I ended up being one of the two students who failed the first Physics exam that year.

At that time, I never imagined that such shortcomings would help me understand and cater to my students' needs in the future and enable me to become a more compassionate professor.

The Jester gene

I am an extrovert by nature. Looking back at my college years, I have vivid memories of my time with my peers, joking around and laughing our hearts away. My jokes earned me the nickname 'Ding' among my friends. How this name came into being is a funny story in itself.

We were coming back to Campus from a late-night movie. During the three-mile walk from the campus gate to the hostels, I was rattling them down to their bones with jokes. Not to brag, but I do think I have a killer sense of humor. This went on until one of them said, "We should not give Anant so many laughs, lest it goes to his head." So it was decided that whenever I cracked a joke, I would have to say 'Ding' to signal the end of the joke, and they could start laughing. The name kind of stuck around.

I never really got enough of making people laugh and being an entertainer. Even through my lectures at MIT, I try to keep the class enthralled with fun tactics to lighten the mood during lessons. For example, you can Google the "chainsaw dance Agarwal", something fun I planned with my Teaching Assistant to help the students better grasp a concept that I was trying to teach in my Electronics course.

Learning is best done through interaction and engagement, and I try to keep both of these levels high during my lectures.

Jack of all. King of none. But better than King of One

I spent a lot of my time participating in a plethora of activities across Campus. I was very much into art, sketching, and painting. I also took part in skits where a number of us would come together and perform extempore. JAMs (just a minute) were one of my favorite activities to participate in. The rest of my spare time was spent playing badminton in the institute courts or table tennis in the Godavari hostel common room. The Mardi Gras campus festival was something that always got me excited each year.

I had been a jack of all trades throughout high school and college. I was interested in a whole lot of things. Everybody kept telling me that I needed to focus. And I should try and become really good at one thing. But I enjoyed doing a lot of things. At that time, I felt like I was somehow doing the wrong thing by not focusing. But it became clear that it does help to engage in a variety of things versus being super good at just one thing.

I also used to play cricket for the high school team. I was the opening bat. That experience helped me realize that life can throw all kinds of balls at once. Sometimes a googly, sometimes a leg-spin, or even an off-spin. If one has the experience, one can tackle them all. One is prepared. The rich and varied experience of doing many things was an advantage because the wide range of experiences helped me in many ways when I got into the business. While growing up, it is essential to keep that in mind. It does not make much sense to try and focus on one thing too early because one never knows what life has in store.

Stanford

All my friends went abroad. I had an internship at the Tata Institute of Fundamental Research in Mumbai. I tried to get into various universities abroad and finally caught my break with Stanford. It was prevalent among IIT graduates, even at those times, to go overseas for post-graduation. I finished my Ph.D. in Electrical Engineering and Computer Science at Stanford and have been teaching students at MIT since then. In the 33 years of my teaching career, I have had numerous students from many of the IITs.

MIT

I work as a professor in the Electrical Engineering and Computer Science department at MIT and have taught thousands of students during my tenure. I was also the Director of CSAIL (MIT's Computer Science & Artificial Intelligence Laboratory).

My time at MIT is where my journey took off. It was the best place for creating startups on the technology side. MIT was very encouraging when it came to independent ventures. I could take a leave of absence or a sabbatical for one or two years, and with the help of my students, get the company on its feet and then return to teaching.

Up until 2011, I was always involved in research work. My students and I immersed ourselves in making discoveries and inventions and publishing them as papers. But just publishing a paper was never enough for me. If one happens to develop new technology, it is one's duty as a researcher to test its utility in the real world. If we stop at writing papers, the technology would just go under the pile unless someone stumbles upon it and finds a use for it somewhere. Once a prototype is built, the next organic step should be to commercialize the technology and make it widely available out there. So if one really wants people to use it and to have an impact, then I firmly believe that one has to start a company or find a way to have people use the technology.

In the startup land, one comes across the factor of usability of a certain technology. One question that repeatedly surfaces is, "How do we best utilize the power of our innovation to make it more accessible and efficient?" Now, I have built five startups along with my students and colleagues during my time at MIT. We would raise money from venture capitalists and hire industry experts. I picked up a lot of business skills on the job. I was comparatively more familiar with the capabilities of our product than with many other aspects of running a business. For example, when I wrote the business plan for my first company, I did not know the difference between marketing and sales! Learning to manage the various aspects of a company is where my versatile experiences came to use. When it comes to making things work, there is no one right way. Through our experiences with different startups, we explored a lot of aspects that go into the making of a company and how to make it work.

For one of our startups, Virtual Machine Works, we had built a prototype of a system that made it very easy to test chips and that too on a large scale. We invented a technology called virtual wires. Those systems are still being used, and some of my students are still at the company building those systems. Units of over one billion dollars worth have likely been sold over the past 25 years.

I spoke to several entrepreneurs. One of my colleagues, Steve Ward, had been an advisor to various startup companies and gave me good advice on how to go about things. He facilitated interaction with a VC who ended up funding the company.

The story about how I got into tech startups as a young faculty member is interesting. I had a chair which was called the Jamieson chair. Burgess Jamieson was a Principal of a VC firm called Sigma Partners. He visited my lab on one occasion, looked at the virtual wires prototype, and said that it was a great idea. He did not end up funding it, but he encouraged me to create a startup.

My student Jonathan Brat was also instrumental in a big way while founding the company. He was a co-founder with me. Charley Selvidge was a former student at MIT who had served as a Teaching Assistant in one of my classes. He ended up being the VP of Engineering. I was initially the CEO, but I hired Allen Michels later on. He had run many companies before and had gained a good reputation for it. We kept building a great team—colleagues, VCs, students, industry experts, and also grew our customers. Starting a company is all about networking and talking. One makes connections and keeps building around them.

The Non-Profit Era

I was on a roll. We were establishing five profit-based companies back to back until the idea for edX came along. We needed it to be focused deeply on the mission and make the right decisions to help humanity. We were clear that we did not want to maximize return on investment and provide for just the investors, but wanted humanity to benefit from it, and hence started out as a non-profit entity. Additionally, it turned out that scaling up to where we are now would not have been possible had we proceeded with a profit-based model. Our goal was to make something that would help propel humanity forward and not just make money.

We made many decisions along the way. Many of those decisions would have been different if we had started out as a for-profit company. For example, we open-sourced our software platform as

Open edX so anyone in the world could download our software for free and use it as they chose to.

Interestingly, I worked harder for this non-profit venture than I had for any of the for-profit companies. I realized with time, money was not as big a motivator as the thought of building something that had an impact on humanity.

How edX came to be

The idea of online learning fascinated me. All my previous startups had been about digitizing physical technology. We had a lot of experience with that, particularly while working on the Virtual Machine world. For years I have been adding digital technology in place of analog components to make systems more reliable, scalable, energy-efficient, and cost-effective. This is what I wanted to do with education as well.

I started by putting up my Electronics Circuits course on MIT open courseware (OCW) in the early 2000s. MIT OCW allowed learners from around the world to access MIT course content freely and was a major pioneer in online learning. We put our recorded classroom videos online along with homework materials and PDFs. However, there was no scope for interaction or discussion forums. Neither did we have labs for an online community, a system to capture feedback, or do grading and certification at that point.

I also felt that technical education would not be meaningful without an online lab. So, around 2000, I began working on an online circuits lab that could be built using digital simulation technology. It can still be found by searching for MIT Websim. I finished building this virtual circuits laboratory around 2003. On an average day, about 300 students from around the world would come and attend the virtual circuits lab. This lab can be called the first MOOC (Massive Open Online Course) lab. It was completely free, open access, scaled to a large number of users, and available for the whole world. I knew I had stepped into something big and that this had massive potential in the virtual education market. This virtual lab prototype also convinced me that we could teach online at scale. Note that this worldwide lab ran on a computer under my desk, and the term cloud computing would only be coined in 2006.

A lot of things started falling into place after that. I was very inspired by Sal Khan (a former student of mine at MIT) in 2008, who had made his videos public. He was making a significant impact with Khan Academy (an American non-profit educational organization). Around 2008–2009, four major technologies arrived hand in hand— Cloud Computing, Video distribution at Scale, Gamification, and Social Networking. All these factors brewed up the perfect storm that ushered in the primordial soup of online learning as we know it today.

Around that time in 2011, I was the Director of MIT CSAIL, the Computer Science and Artificial Intelligence Laboratory at MIT. There was a meeting where MIT leadership and the Deans had all gathered to discuss the future of MIT and education in general. There were many suggestions about international expansion, for example, starting a new campus in Bangalore or the Middle East. When my turn came, I argued that creating a new campus was like running for a single in cricket (Cricket analogies are a force of habit with me). Rather than opening one new Campus, why don't we create a virtual MIT for the whole world? It will be like hitting a sixer. Everybody laughed. However, Rafael Reif, the then Provost of MIT and current President of MIT, called me up and said, "Let's do it." He and other MIT leaders had been thinking along similar lines, and I got massive support from him and the MIT leadership to put up this project.

Around 2011, we began discussing at MIT the possibilities of putting some of our courses online for the whole world in a way that goes well beyond MIT Open Courseware. I had a virtual circuits lab that proved that we could do virtual circuits at scale. Then there was Sal Khan, who had put up his videos online and demonstrated that engaging learning at a large scale is possible. It would also incorporate discussion forums and an MIT certificate for learners who successfully manage to complete the course.

We came up with a website that would make MIT accessible to the whole world. We code-named it MITx. The x stood for the standard symbol. We used it as a variable that could take any value. So x could be an answer, x could be infinity, or stand for the experience. That is the sort of openness that we were aiming for.

The First Course

We announced MITx on December 19, 2011. And my first course was up by February the following year.

Meanwhile, MIT and Harvard leaders had been in conversation regarding partnering on this online education venture. In this regard, I remember my good friend, the EVP of Finance at MIT then, Israel Ruiz. He and I put in an all-nighter to create a financial spreadsheet and a business plan. We budgeted 60 million dollars and approached MIT and Harvard to pitch in. Harvard and MIT did team up to make this happen. The whole thing came together very well. When Harvard came in, we became edX in early May of 2012.

Initially, in late 2011, we wanted to launch a Computer Science course as the first MITx course by late January 2012, but Faculty colleagues whom I approached felt that it could not be done in such a short window. Since we had already announced MITx, I decided to launch my Circuits and Electronics course as the first course. We had virtual labs and some course materials. Additionally, my colleague Jacob White made a simulation-based, high-speed differential equation solver. Chris Terman built a new virtual circuits lab which was powered by White's equation solver. Jerry Sussman developed many of the problem sets.

We began hiring a small team, including our first hire Piotr Mitros, a former student of mine at MIT, who began developing the platform. Piotr and I sketched out the pedagogy of the platform—active learning—and wireframes for interactions on the whiteboard in my CSAIL office. We also brainstormed how the various learning engagement components, including videos, discussions, problem set grading, labs, and certification, would fit together into a system. This was when we came up with the idea of a discussion board integrated within the online learning platform as part of the learning experience. We also sketched out the learning user interface (UI) and the concept of learning sequences which remains in the edX platform, even to this day, 10 years later. It was a fantastic team effort, and it was exciting to see it all come together.

When all these preparations were in motion, the President of MIT, Susan Hockfield, expressed a worry. She had apprehensions that the course's enrollment might be disappointing and that we would get only 20-30 students for a circuits course. She felt we would have been in a safer position if we had launched a CS course. I explained the problem to her. At that point, the only thing we could do was to wait and watch how the world responded.

We designed the course having 200 to 2000 takers in mind. To our surprise, we had over ten thousand people enrolling in the first hour of the website going up. Now we were faced with the opposite problem. How do we scale up?

Incidentally, the beauty of cloud computing lies in that one can add in a bunch of virtual machines and scale in real-time. More than 1.5 lakh students from 162 countries signed up for this first offering of a hard MIT course before we even knew it. This was more than the total number of MIT alumni in its 150-year history. 7200 students passed the course, which is also a big number. It was more than the number of students I had taught at MIT in my teaching career of 33 years.

Why MOOCs are so impactful

Our millennial generation is built differently. Our children interact with the world very differently than we used to do. They are entirely comfortable with online technology. So why are we fighting it in the classrooms? We should embrace it and make the most of it.

Several important aspects of modern online learning enhance learner engagement, such as active learning, instant feedback, gamification, and discussion forums.

Active learning is one of the key ideas here. Rather than driving kids into the classroom at 8 a.m. for three to four hours of lectures, have them watch five to ten videos. The instructors can create interleaved sequences of videos and interactive exercises called learning sequences. A learning sequence replaces a lecture. It gives the student the option of self-paced learning and makes the course much more interactive than is ever possible in an offline setting.

MOOCs offer instant feedback through the capabilities of the Internet. The computer grades the exercises, and students can correct their mistakes in real-time rather than waiting for the professor to finish grading for the entire class. The green checkmark is becoming one of the most significant symbols for edX. The students get instant gratification upon getting the correct answers, and that incentive drives them to learn further.

Gamification is, quite literally, a game-changer in the field of online learning. This is what made online laboratories possible. The students interact with real-life representations of the concepts they are learning and can try out different combinations to get different results, just like they can in a game. It helps build a more comprehensive understanding of the concepts at hand. It is hands-on and enables the student to build a world around the core theories.

Our website's discussion forums also encourage peer-learning and foster communication skills among the students. There have been instances where a student posted a doubt on one of my courses, and before I could answer it, numerous other students from all over the world jumped in and attempted to solve that doubt. In the end, they got the answer right, and all I had to do was bless the answer—"good answer." I had not realized the humongous revolution this form of learning would bring about until I saw this peer-learning unfold in real-time.

The Great Convergence

Over the years, a lot more universities came together to join edX. We hosted courses from the University of California Berkeley, University of Texas Austin and Arlington, Boston University, and the University of Maryland. The edX model grew. Today we have more than 170 institutional partners—Cambridge University, Oxford University, IIM Bangalore, IIT Bombay, among many others. We also have several leading corporations such as IBM, Linux Foundation, Google, Amazon, etc., as our partners. Entire nations also joined as partners, including Israel and Afghanistan.

edX Alumni

Amol Bhave, a high school student from Jabalpur, took my first course on edX and did exceptionally well. I wrote him a recommendation letter. He ended up attending MIT. When he was in his third year, I experimented with my online circuits course among the MIT campus students, where about half the students took the online course, and half the students took the in-person campus course. He had already done the course online much before he came to MIT. So he just took the online exam, and he aced it. He went on to work at Facebook.

Beraki Befekadu, an edX learner who lived as a refugee in Nigeria, was interested in Computer Engineering. But due to his financial constraints, he had to drop out of school and took up a job as an Internet Cafe attendant. He hoped to become a software developer someday and wanted to buy his parents a house. Upon discovering edX, he enrolled for the Harvard CS50 course. After that, he earned a scholarship at Makerere University for pursuing a BS in Computer Science. Beraki now works as a software developer in Canada.

The other side of MOOCs

While learners were opting for fully online courses, some teachers also adopted our courses as an aid in their classrooms in many innovative ways. One way we came to know about this was from a blog two such teachers wrote. Two high school teachers at Sant High school in Ulaanbaatar, Mongolia, had flipped the classroom. Under these teachers' guidance, 15-year-olds in this high school used the video lectures and exercises and learned online from this course, which was ideally designed for undergraduate students. The students would then come to the classroom and have discussions and do laboratory exercises in person.

This blended learning method combining online and classroom teaching further bridged the engagement gap that one might have faced if learning was solely through an online platform. Healthy interaction among peers also made a big difference in such learning experiences. This learning method is now called blended learning or hybrid learning.

Our revenue model

We are now scaling and applying these blended learning pilots in several universities and high schools around the world. This also solves a practical problem of MOOCs, which is the business aspect. We work with universities all around the world to offer our MOOCs so that professors can use these online courses in their classrooms or just use them as another tool in their arsenal, much like they use a textbook. edX has even built a product called edX Online Campus to be able to support this initiative at colleges and universities.

While almost all courses on edX are available with an audit track where students can learn for free, we also offer learners the option to pay a fee in order to earn a certificate that verifies that they have completed a course on edX. These are authentic certificates from some of the most recognized universities and corporations around the world and can be a great addition to an aspiring learner's CV.

As our model grew more extensive, we started hosting stackable, modular credentials on edX. These first of their kind credentials, called MicroMasters programs, were piloted by MIT and edX and were launched in September 2016. They were groundbreaking in terms of expanding access to graduate-level education. We also launched Professional Certificate programs for upskilling and reskilling for the future workplace.

In 2017, Georgia Tech's Master of Science in Analytics paved the way for affordable online Master's degrees in edX that built upon a MicroMasters program. Today we have several degrees on edX, including a $10K Master's degree in Computer Science and Data Science from UT Austin, as well as a $24K MBA from the Questrom School of Business at Boston University.

And in 2020, we launched the first-ever credit-backed, stackable online credential—a MicroBachelors program, giving learners a pathway to earn a full bachelor's degree.

Chapter 12

Start with Why Not

Satish Kannan: MediBuddy

The first thought which comes to my mind when I think of Satish is "Disciplined Hyper-scaling". Building an organization with 1000+ employees, a partner network of over 90,000 doctors, 7000 hospitals, 3000 diagnostic centers, and 2500 pharmacies in such a short span of time. The chapter goes in-depth to explain how he built these skills while exploring the love story between him and the Health-Tech industry from his campus time.

The first year is always a relief

Before joining the institute, I was in those exhausting JEE Factories (Insti lingo for coachings), studying day and night in Bangalore. After joining IIT, I had some time on my plate to spend playing football in Jamuna Quadrangle. Enba (Co-founder) used to live two rooms next to mine. We were classmates, wingmates, batchmates, and both were dual-degree guys.

Experimenting the science

During October-November, Shaastra happened, which lit up the spark for technology inside me. This happened because of the "Spirit of Engineering (SOE)". Under SOE projects, all students had to come together and do a large scale highly technically challenging project, like putting a fire brigade on the fourth floor of the Admin

Block. So, in my first year, it was a Quadcopter. It had four motors, and it went up and came down. Although it looks like a very simple thing now and just one Amazon delivery away, in 2007, that was a very new concept. It totally blew me up. This sparked my interest to another level. I started enquiring about who made these, and I came to know it was the CFI (Centre for Innovation). I met them and chatted with them, and they said, "If you are so interested, why don't you join us?"

Joining Shaashtra and taking it ahead

By the end of the first year, I became a volunteer for the spirit of an engineering project for the next year. Their project was called "Want To Fly". In our second year, we planned on building an RC-controlled automated Aircraft. It would be a small aircraft, taking off and landing on its own. But there was a problem—the project was to cost 6 lakhs. So, we went to the Dean of Students (DoSt) and gave a whole presentation about how amazing it will be. He looked excited, but as soon as we started listing what we wanted, he started staring at us. As soon as we said it would cost 6 lakhs, he was kind of surprised.

We all started explaining to DoSt. He was somewhat convinced. However, he couldn't invest the entire money due to certain reasons. So, he connected us with the Dean ICSR, who gave us some of the money, and we all came to an agreement where we'll be making as many parts as possible by ourselves. The rest would be taken care of by them.

This taught me two major learnings about being at IIT. First, it gives you a lot of freedom. Second, it also gives you related resources to experiment and innovate.

After seven months—from February to September—of hard work, our fabulous plane was ready. It was flying and landing properly. But then, a mishap happened. Just three days before the show, we were doing trials. It took a great take-off, but while it was in mid-air, we saw one of its parts falling from the sky. Then we saw the plane falling straight down, and boom, it was broken into small pieces. I literally started shouting like, "*KYA*, why is this happening with us?" I freaked out since deals were done, slots were fixed, and it was one of the prime attractions.

Now, this came as the biggest challenge for the whole Shaastra team. For the next three days, 15 teams worked day in day out, not napping even for a single hour. A few guys were so tired that they slept off while standing. But the hard work finally paid off. We presented our plane, and it did a fantastic job.

This just didn't help me learn how to work with a team, but it made me ready to face the worst situations.

Jumping into competitions

With our exponentially increasing interest in technology, we started participating in as many competitions as possible. We participated in institute competitions like Mechanica (By the Mechanical Department), Amalgam (By the Metallurgy Department), Wavez (By Nav Arch. Department), etc. But didn't win any of them.

Then, a competition took place—TIDAC, TEXAS INSTRUMENTS ANALOGUE DESIGN CHALLENGE. The winners would get prize money of $10K.

We were very eager to take part in the same. That time Enba, Ananthanarayanan, and I were in our fourth year. We were excited and started working hard to win the competition. Our project was "Low-Cost Integrated Wireless Health Monitoring System with Emergency Response". This was our first dive into Health-tech. We interacted with Doctors and Patients day in and day out. We understood their problems and the solutions we could offer. Our hard work paid off, and we won the competition.

This didn't just bring us money, but also a good amount of publicity. DoSt (Dean of Students) and our HoD (Head of Department) even wrote letters mentioning us, and this got us recognized by one of our professors Ashok Jhujhunwala (The major guy behind building the Incubation Cell at IIT Madras.)

Small money is big in college

In the final year of our dual degree, we had ample time on hand. My dear friend Enba and I started doing some freelancing work during that time. We wanted to taste the hands-on part of technology and gain some real-time experience. We used our technological skills to work in real-life industries. We built software and technology solutions for small businesses.

Continuing the passion in Job

During our placements, we had options like going to companies like ITC in the management space or McKinsey in the consulting space. I even did an internship at Intel in chip development. However, it wasn't my calling. Also, after working on the TIDAC project, our interest in health care just kept increasing. At that time, there were just two major companies from healthcare—Philips Healthcare and GE Healthcare.

I joined Philips Healthcare. At the same time, Enba got a job in Qualcomm, although he declined it and went to work at Healthcare Technology Innovation Centre (HTIC) at IITM Research Park. It was a healthcare-focused incubation center where he was working on diabetes-related problems. They used AI to check its effect on your eyes and to prevent blindness from that. While in Philips, I started working on heart-related machines that help angioplasty.

0, 0.5, 1 Go

At that time, there weren't any institute entrepreneurs to look up to; there were people from the 80s and 90s who used to come and give lectures, and there was someone special in them. In 2011, Anand, the man behind Junglee, came to give a lecture at IITM. I took him on a tour of the institute and showed him our projects. Little did I know that he would be our biggest supporter back then.

But after some time, I started getting the feeling of doing something which could have a bigger impact. So, I decided to leave Philips and do my own startup. At that time, my dad was working in Bangalore. He got pretty worried since I was doing well working in Philips. There were a lot of worries, but I really wanted to do that.

In 2013, after working for a year in the companies we joined, Enba and I decided to quit our jobs and planned to start something of our own. So, we came back to the campus, but we didn't have a clue on how to start it. So, I reached out to Prof. Jhunjhunwala. He gave us a couple of tables in one of his labs and asked us to start working from there. We stayed in a rented house in Velachery, since we couldn't get hostels. The first year was tough. We didn't have much money, just our savings. But to support our startup, IIT Madras gave us an investment of Rs. 5 lakhs. Since the research park was getting started, we used to just stay in labs all day. Our initial product was a hardware ECG machine based on IoT (Internet of Things). Initially, we used to go in and around Chennai to nearby hospitals, Stanley Medical college, and other Diagnostic Centers, talking to doctors. While working at Philips, I had interacted with a lot of doctors. Since they had seen me from Philips, they trusted me.

As for building our team, we started hiring interns from the institute. I used to drop mails with the subject "Invitations for Interns". And so, many enthusiastic 2nd, 3rd, and 4th-year students applied. Since we didn't have much money to give, we used to take them to Tiffany's (now Usha), buy them Egg Fried Rice, and coke, and they used to work from evening 6 to 2 at night. After some time, when we started having money, we started giving them incentives.

Our first product was minimal, yet we kept building it. Then, we stopped on hardware and worked only on software.

Our initial hardware was focused on cardiology. When we started talking to doctors, we understood that we could help larger numbers of patients over and above just cardiology using our software platform, although the hardware was only cardiology focused.

In order to help a larger base, we moved to software.

Anand Rajaraman gave us advice, "Digital tech in India is going to boom, and for mobile and internet, 2013 is the gateway. Let's also focus on that."

Once our software was ready, we started reaching out to doctors. Physical intervention is a very crucial part of the check-up.

A person from a small village had to travel a lot to just meet a good doctor from cities like Chennai, Delhi, and Mumbai. We requested the doctors, saying, "These people already live so far away. Why don't you use our software?"

In case they liked it, we asked them if they could refer it to their doctor friends. They could just call and say, "This boy is from IIT. I liked his software; just give it a shot." This mouth-to-mouth publicity helped us in scaling. Getting the first 40 doctors was the toughest. Telemedicine was new then, but doctors weren't using it that much. Because it's like you had to have a big computer. Doctors are using webcams now. By the time we started, the mobile phone had done the whole job.

We worked for two years, and things started getting better by then. We started surviving.

High Output Growth

Initially, we gave free consultations. Then, we moved to paid consultation. When you are a very small company, you should not worry about the competition much. You should worry about the product-market fit. Everything has to be done according to the customer's needs and demands.

Initially, numerous small firms had the same idea, but our worry was the customer and problems in healthcare. Once you start becoming big, whoever scales fast is the winner. In every situation, you have to find a way to grow faster. For scaling fast, talk to the customer, try to know what more problems he has, and solve them. Initially, the app was just in English. Then, it was released in Hindi too. Doctors used to talk only in just English then. Now, they speak 16 languages.

At all points of time, you have to keep upping your game. We started scaling vertically too. We started selling medicines and labs. In our field, currently, we are the largest player—scale, revenue, employee base, largest investment—in everything.

Introducing MediBuddy

All startups need to grow super-fast, and we should make a decision on consolidating the market very early. When I was growing DocsApp, MediBuddy was also providing similar services. We thought it would be great to bring both together and build a larger company to help more Indians.

In June 2020, to create market leadership in the digital healthcare industry, DocsApp (India's leading online doctor consultation platform) merged with MediBuddy. Going forward, both MediBuddy and DocsApp will operate under a single brand name—MediBuddy.

Today, MediBuddy serves the healthcare needs of over three crore Indians with a partner network of over 90,000 doctors, 7000 hospitals, 3000 diagnostic centers, and 2500 pharmacies, covering over 95% of all pin codes in India.

Brief Chronicles 3

Ravishankar G Shiroor,
M.Tech, Electrical Engineering — Batch of 1996.
Co-founder, Director, Stellapps Technologies

Stellapps is an internationally acclaimed farm to consumer dairy-digitization service provider, improving productivity, quality and ensuring end-to-end traceability across the dairy supply chain. It leverages advanced analytics and artificial intelligence through its full-stack IoT platform to enable dairy ecosystem partnerships with financial and insurance institutions, veterinary services, cattle nutrition providers, etc., to drive significant value for each stakeholder, including smallholder farmers. Through its customer base, which includes all major private and cooperative dairies, Stellapps currently digitizes over 13 million liters of milk, worth USD 3.4 million, each day and impacts 2.8 million dairy farmers in over 36,000 Indian villages.

We at Stellapps started our entrepreneurial journey in 2011 with the vision of "applying M2M and IoT technology" to the sectors relevant to the Indian Economy. After working in the then-booming IT industry for 15 years, my co-founders and I decided to found a startup. With only a few startup examples, the startup sector was not popular then. The startup ecosystem was also just getting established. Even our families doubted our decision to quit our well-paying jobs to set up a startup company. The support from IIT Madras gave us the impetus to grow Stellapps to what it is now.

We first approached IIT Madras for funding support for our dairy customers. Although the Indian dairy industry is number one globally, more than 99% of the Indian dairy farmers are at the bottom of the pyramid. Hence, the Indian dairy industry was unsure of its ability to pay for technology interventions in the dairy farms. We approached RTBI (Rural Technology and Business Incubator at IIT Madras) to check if we could get some funding support for our customers to buy our technology. The RTBI team and Professor Jhunjhunwala instead expressed interest in investment support for Stellapps.

The IITM-RTBI incubator served as a launchpad for Stellapps. We connected to industry leaders and government agencies and even presented our solutions to the Hon' PM, Shri. Narendra Modi. Some of our largest customers were through introductions made by IITM. We were lucky to be mentored by Professor Jhunjhunwala and leaders like Thiru. Murugappan Sir, who is part of a mentoring program at RTBI. The Director of IIT Madras, Dr. Bhaskar Ramamurthy, has often been in touch with us. We were elated when he took the time to visit us at a dairy farm in Tamil Nadu.

Words cannot express the immense contribution of my alma-mater, IIT Madras, in my life. The solid technical foundation I built while at IITM helped me become a better engineer. Much later, the support received from IIT Madras and RTBI shaped my career as an entrepreneur. Apart from the learnings at the institute and the great professors, I made lifelong friends, some of whom even invested at an early stage in Stellapps. I would like to thank Prof. Jhunjhunwala, Dr. Ramamurthy, and IIT Madras profusely for all their contributions to my professional journey and for helping millions of Indian dairy farmers gain access to life-changing technology interventions by investing their time and resources in Stellapps.

Chapter 13

We Did Start the Fire

Albin Jose: Lal10

Picture a 2 BHK apartment in Bangalore, housing three bachelors. In itself, the flat is perfectly ordinary with the scattered belongings, unwashed laundry, and dishes in the sink left unattended—a typical bachelor's apartment.

The corner room hosts a tenant to keep up with the costs. This flat serves as their makeshift office/living quarters. You know how hard it is to find a decent place in Bangalore! The occupants of this house *appear* to be just as typical and mundane. One of them is a quiet guy who sits at his desk at the corner of the hall room.

Now, let's speed things up a bit. Three years down the lane, our quiet guy and his two other flatmates were covered in **30Under30 Forbes, raising over $1.5M in funding**. They achieved this feat by revolutionizing the supply of authentic handcrafted artisan products from India with their initiative, **Lal10.**

Lal10 acts as a vital bridge that helps artisans' businesses and brings the trust factor within the consumer pool. The Lal10 team is working toward eliminating the baneful and bringing out the real Bharat's best products in stores like Zara and Fab India.

One of the critical pillars of this bridge is Albin Jose, **aka Bhavandar,** a Metallurgy student from Narmada. Albin is that friend in a group who makes everyone laugh, but people barely know him outside your group. Even he refers to himself as the "Guy lying at the peak of the bell curve." (I believe he means to say absolutely average, but we don't believe that.)

He humorously recalled his early college days:

Life at IITM

Turbulent Initial years

Initially, I wanted to top all my classes and attend all the lectures. A typical starry-eyed student that comes to an IIT. But *ek saal ke baad sab line pe agaya (everything became clear after the firsts year)*. **MA101 (The first course in the mathematics discipline)** made me realize that engineering is going to be one tough nut to crack.

But IITs are brimming with all sorts of colorful personalities. I really found my *jam* in **Word Games**. So, I was an active participant of the word games club and represented **Narmada Hostel** in LitSoc a couple of times. The best part about that time was making new friends and finding people with similar interests. There were a lot of activities to explore, like drama, LitSoc, etc. I was overwhelmed at first, but it was a very exciting experience. It was a turbulent time for me, as the first year is for most people. I did not have a clear sense of purpose. But it yielded a lot of happy memories.

College PORs

I had that *enthu freshie* attitude throughout my first year. After goofing around a bit, in the second year, I took up the responsibility for General Arrangements for **Shaastra**. I was still trying out stuff, figuring out responsibilities. Even though it was a famous and high-demand POR, I realized that it was not the sort of work I wanted to do.

I learned from my shortcomings and tried to take on bigger responsibilities in my third year.

That was when I learned a lot—sending applications, reaching out to companies, and initiating deals to raise money for **Saarang** as a Sponsorship Coordinator. I also worked on raising funds for my hostel as an Alumni Affairs Secretary. I had finally found a place where I could exercise my people skills.

Through these PORs, I cultivated my strengths in getting people/companies on board, which laid a strong foundation for what was to come in the future. Along with this, my involvement in the Institute elections taught me a lot about working with people from different sections of society.

A shot at the Core field

With all of this going on, I did put up a fight in metallurgy (my core field) for the initial three years because of two major reasons:

1. Because I was studying in one of the top-notch engineering colleges in India.

2. My professor, Dr. Phani Kumar.

Phani Sir always encouraged me to put up a fight. He used to call me to his office and lecture me for hours about improving my performance and trying more for the core.

To ascertain if I really was into core, I took up an internship in the Meta industry in my 3rd year at **Tube Investments** in Avadi, where I traveled from campus every day.

Although I wasn't very aligned toward the core field, I decided to give it the shot it deserved. *Tabhi socha tha ki BTP (B.Tech Project) me fight maarenge and core me kuch feel laayenge.* (I had thought at that time that I'll put fight to complete BTP and get the feel of being in metallurgy.) Despite this, I could not bring myself to complete my BTP, and I opted for courses instead. At that time, it did feel like a great loss **not having done my BTP**. I had friends who had worked spectacularly on their BTP, and I felt a little left out of the action. But in retrospect, I am glad I made that decision. I know now that it would have served as nothing more than another point on my resume.

Not doing my BTP gave me time to explore different directions that my career could take before placements. By the fourth year, my whole focus was on getting a job, making some money. I thought of doing an MBA after that, maybe. I'll have another shot at academics and maybe, *redeem myself* somehow. It could be like a Hail Mary pass for me. Because I realized that a core job was not exactly my cup of tea. (Imagine realizing this after spending four years in your core field.)

From coaching to social entrepreneurship

Coming from a family of teachers, I thought to try my hand at teaching by joining an entrance-level coaching institute. Initially, my mom was not very happy at the prospect of my teaching. As a former teacher, she knew that what you get in return as a teacher is very non-tangible. She was understandably skeptical about it.

It's not a very glamorous profession. **But education is important**. My mother is a teacher, and my grandfather was a government school Headmaster. I have a lot of respect for the teaching community, and that is why I decided to go forward with my decision.

Teaching came very naturally to me, and we were paid decently. But I realized quite early on that the culture at coaching institutes was not for me. Post this, I took up a position at **AVANTI Learning Centres**.

It is a social venture that creates cost-effective educational opportunities for students from the lower middle class using a peer-learning pedagogy. A lot of these students get admitted into good engineering colleges. I was a part of the small team designing the curriculum for these kids. It wasn't exactly classroom teaching, but it had all aspects I liked about it.

I really liked the social angle of this job. That was my first initiation toward social entrepreneurship. I got first-hand experience in making a difference. Working at the lower rung of the Pyramid, I made a lot of difference.

At AVANTI, I learned to work from the ground up and built the foundations of a structure that will help people for years to come. I was introduced to the idea of social entrepreneurship and realized how much of a difference I could make in society. I knew then that I had so much more to give.

Entrepreneurship was not really an option for me at the time. But the wheels had already been set in motion.

It is important to know what you want. But it is equally important to realize when something is not compatible with you. I knew when to let go of stuff, which eventually led me to find what I was meant for without regretting it. I did not leave room for "What if?"

Lal10

The chords struck when I met Maneet and Sanchit in Mumbai. We met when Maneet had held a small exhibition for handicrafts, which turned out to be a huge success. The year was 2014, and the events leading to the foundation of Lal10 were set in motion.

Entrepreneurship was not a planned journey for me. I serendipitously (fortunately, with a stroke of luck) got into it. Maneet showed me the potential of this industry and what work needed to be done. He showed me the numbers, and it was all clear. Handicrafts were the second-largest rural employment-generating sector in India after agriculture.

Agriculture gets a lot of spotlight. But crafts are an industry that has always been operated remotely in the shadows. I saw the gap in the industry and could see us filling that gap. I had never given entrepreneurship a thought before this. But my conversation with Maneet opened a lot of doors for me, and I was exposed to the immense potential this sector holds. Sourcing handicrafts was a whole new world just waiting to be explored.

There are two kinds of people. There are the ones who know what they want to do and are willing to work for it. Then, there are others who keep trying different stuff until they find the right thing for them. I belonged to the second category. My advice to the latter would be to explore wholeheartedly and choose wisely from all the things you have tried out. I had tried out a lot of things before joining Lal10, and my parents were slightly concerned that I was not going the right way. I had to believe in myself then. *Thoda sa darr to tha yaar. Par uss time socha ki bas kaam par lag jaate hai. (I was certainly a little bit scared, but at that time I just thought let me just focus on doing the work.)* I knew something about this felt right, and I decided to proceed with it. It was the best decision I ever made.

I left work for Avanti around October 2015. (Lal10 was just a website then.) I moved to Bangalore along with Maneet and Sanchit. Those were initial turbulent days, and the venture was yet to take off. We were patiently hoping to break through with the revenue. By February, all three of us wrapped up our other obligations and started working full-time toward Lal10.

Initially, I worked with artisan onboarding, which involved a lot of traveling. These products usually have a small supply chain, already established if a particular craft is famous enough. But the whole sector is largely unorganized. Our aim was not to disrupt the existing chains but to make them more centralized and ensure the artisans get the right price for their products. All of us were working on the ground at first, but we soon realized that this would not be sustainable. We needed to find a more scalable option. So, we came up with a rather *clever hack.*

We reached out to the students of NIFTs. We knew that they had to interact with artisan clusters in and around their institute as part of their curriculum. By getting interns from NIFTs spread all across India, we had the perfect way to onboard these artisans. So, we shot out emails to these institutes and hired a bunch of interns to work with us. Things were picking up pace. As we got more and more interns involved, we could see things falling into place.

The first intern that we had on board was one such student. He came over to our office/apartment in Bangalore to work with us. He also got a place in Koramangala. It was a refreshing experience to get to see a fresh face in the office apart from us three every morning. That was a very welcome change.

Another key factor was that mega clusters (a collection of villages that practiced a variety of crafts) like Kachh or Moradabad often had their own WhatsApp groups. These groups could really help us connect with artisans from all over these mega clusters without going there. There were certain gaps, but technology made it so much easier. Our team made sure that we were making optimal use of all resources.

At present, we have a full-fledged team working for artisan onboarding and sourcing. It has grown a lot from the small hacks that we implemented initially. But those were very important steps from India to Bharat.

Our ethos was based on eliminating the traditional middleman and getting the artisans the prices they deserve.

It all worked out well after establishing authentic sourcing and building on a loyal consumer base. We started gaining consumers organically.

The transition from B2C to B2B

We still could not break through with our B2C model despite our progress. Lal10 was in need of a revamped business model.

The **B2C** model was not generating enough revenue. We were earning only a few thousands per month, and it was not a welcoming prospect. Some occasional odd deals brought in some revenue, but we needed a more sustainable revenue flow. We gathered a portion of inventories from the artisans and went to sell the stock early in the mornings. We sub-let the apartment's backroom to someone to make up for Lal10's costs. It was a very grim situation.

The biggest problem we faced in B2C was the lack of live inventory tracking. We needed to check in periodically with the artisans about whether or not they had inventory to meet the order's requirements. It was a loss of opportunity for the artisans and a lack of reliable supply for the consumers, which led to mutual discontent. It was a lose-lose situation.

There have been trust deficits within suppliers as well as customers. There were cases where the middleman cheated the artisans, and they never saw payment for the goods they produced. At other times, we heard of customers that were cheated by artisans and lost a lot of money. Our vision was to step in right there and sort of bridge this trust gap, specifically in B2B, which involves a large consignment of orders.

When we won the IIT Bplan Competition Eureka, one of our judges was Mr. CHAND DAS. He was the ex-CEO of the ITC stationery division and one of the pioneers of the Classmate brand.

He started mentoring us pro bono. He had strong experience in implementing and perfecting rural supply chain models through the E-Choupal initiative of ITC. He had worked hands-on with the rural sector throughout his career. He introduced a new concept to us. He said we could generate more days of livelihood for these artisans in addition to more revenue overall if we shift from B2C to B2B. There are a lot of people who want to maintain consistent production. So, facilitating large consignments will completely change the game.

When we tried B2B, we successfully turned the tables to make it a win-win for all the parties involved. Large consignments are mainly ordered and not taken directly from the inventory. So, when a brand comes in and orders 100 pieces, it's much more profitable for the artisan because he is getting a business for a hundred pieces and will be more willing to invest time in it. It also fetches them a more sustainable livelihood. As for the customers, they are happy with the products from authentic artisans and are saved from the hassle of having to find sources. So, they keep coming back for the service.

I finally felt like we had kicked off in the right direction when B2B took off for us. When we managed to create a sustainable supply chain in the industry, revenue started growing.

The path to funding

Funding is one of the key moments in the journey of every startup. Lal10 has been able to raise about $1.1 M in their seed round in March 2020. We had also managed to raise $400,000 from our angel investors. Our first angel investor was Mr. Chand Das.

I was the one that reached out to Mr. T.T. Jagannathan. I dropped a cold email to his office email id, pitching our work and investing prospects. He did not take long to make his decision to invest in Lal10.

It took a lot of effort until we reached the seed round for angel investors.

It is the initial rounds of funding that are the trickiest. You are a completely new presence in the investment market without any prior statistics to back your ability to return on investments. You have to build your credibility from the ground up. A company really has to prove itself in all aspects. This is where you have to demonstrate how your solution is good for the market and establish your place. After the first round, you could continue and grow organically.

We plan to scale to international markets and use this funding to create a stronger technology base for their service.

Future Prospects

Our main focus for the future is to reach out to small boutiques and brands internationally. We are launching our marketplace by the end of September 2020. It will be a transactional model where artisans can also list their inventories. Thanks to Covid, we have a lot of inventory stocked up. Many of these small brands are expected to buy assortments. So, we are working on that functionality for our platform.

To manage transactions on the artisan's end, we are trying to develop a chat-based model so that they can monitor their orders conveniently. Since we realized that many of them are familiar with WhatsApp, we are trying to build an app with similar functionality to ease use.

Competitors and strategies

Our biggest competitors in B2B are export houses that operate in their own individual silos in dealing internationally. These guys focus mostly on bulk international orders. But they fail to recognize the immense potential in domestic markets. Sourcing is a major concern for small business owners who are scattered all across the country. They cannot send large teams to look for sources. Brands into handcrafted products' retail, like **Fab India,** are predominantly retail B2C models, and we consider them more as our allies than competitors. Some of them are our customers as well.

The People – The Journey

As promising and fulfilling as this journey has been, I will be lying if I say I didn't feel doubtful about it at times. But as a team, we always talked and sorted things out. Maneet and Sanchit have always helped me see the bright side of things. I think Maneet is highly optimistic (as CEOs have to be). I am more of a realist. As for Sanchit, he is the most pragmatic of us all. So, we all fit in together very well.

I remember my parents being really proud when I was featured in Forbes. They were finally relieved *ki chalo kuch toh achaa kar raha hai yeh.* (Okay, at least he is doing something good.) I had backlash from those typical relatives who never really believed in what I was doing. But there were points when all of their apprehensions were put to dirt.

Coming from a person who did not have an inkling about entrepreneurship when being in a college with a history of producing stellar entrepreneurs,

If you really feel an idea can bring about change and you see yourself working toward that change, you should go for it. But implementation is very important. Or else, it is just a passing thought. One very important quality that explorers like me must possess is the ability to drop a dead idea. Sometimes, we hold onto an idea like it's a baby. We should face the truth about our mistakes and learn from them. It's difficult, but it is a must if you want to survive as a company.

Chapter 14

The Disruptor's Phenomena

Tanmai Gopal: CEO and Founder of Hasura

Tanmai is one of the most straightforward people I have met in my life, and that feature passes on the way he lives life and does Entrepreneurship—a crystal-clear set of thoughts and visions while cherishing the process of trials. Another feature that makes him stand out is his strong sense of responsibility toward people.

Early Notions about Science

I have long since had this inkling to start something of my own. But I was not familiar with the notions of a startup per se. But the idea of creating something from scratch and for it to have an impact was always an ebbing desire.

As a teenager, I was very intrigued by the sciences because they had always fascinated me. There was something very inanely elegant about the first principle that governed the world around us. I found myself spellbound.

But when it comes to making a decision, every child is faced with a dilemma. Which path should I take?

My parents were under the impression that engineering is pretty much like science, except it's more in demand in the industry. This was only partly true, but what did I know then? I relented. Computer Science was very attractive to me because it seemed like we'd created an entire unconstrained universe of possibilities on top of a physically constrained reality. I had no idea how things worked, and that's what I wanted to learn more about.

And so began my Journey at IITM.

The IITM Journey

The pull of CSE

What really fascinated me about CSE was that it was a new field. It was a whole new world with its own rules built on the same first principles as everything else. In school, you learn a lot of underlying science behind other fields, but not about computer science. So, in a way, CS is like a magical entity that humans have built up from the more real and tangible laws of physics. And as a student with no prior knowledge of how it works, it was like standing at the shore of an infinite ocean that calls for you to dive in.

Abstraction. That's a very important word. That is what pulled me toward CSE. And it was very unfortunate that coming into an IIT, I had no notion whatsoever about this amazing field. It's not like that in other parts of the world. Students there spend a lot more time trying to figure out what it is that they want to do before pursuing higher education. Sometimes, students also get some work experience before going into that field. That kind of passion-driven choice is what gives you the energy to pursue your field further.

But here, we have it all reversed. First, we decide, and then we wait to get inspired, which doesn't always work out. But fortunately, it did for me. My objective was always to cover as much breadth as possible and explore all the possibilities in CSE. I embraced the subjects. I learned with an open mind.

And I really liked what I studied. I won't say I was very academically inclined, but I was very curious. This set of beliefs enabled me to focus on my interests more. The transition to not viewing everything solely from an academic performance perspective was very refreshing.

College extracurriculars

During my time at Insti, I was involved in a lot of other things. I injected myself into different kinds of groups. I was never heavily involved in the Tech clubs, but I did take part in Lit Soc initially. I also did my minor in social entrepreneurship and innovation—a new minor at the time—and made a lot of friends from different engineering branches, management studies, and the humanities department. I loved my humanities electives as well, from German to Design History.

I was an events coordinator during **Shaastra** in my third year. Although I did have a lot of fun doing this work and meeting a lot of people with different worldviews, a real downer for me during that time was that people kept talking about their resumes. I could not fathom why it was so much of a concern for them. Because for me, it was always like this. I did stuff that I was into, and that was what my resume showed—my interests. Doing something just for the resume seemed like a very reductionist point of view. It never agreed with me.

The most material impact of the time was the people I met. For example, I met Anand during my **Shaastra** events POR. He was a core member too. We became really good friends, and we stayed in touch. Later, he joined me to become a part of the founding team of **Hasura**.

Those kinds of experiences were interesting. You learn a lot about people, and you learn a lot about yourself. You learn about how to lead people and how to talk to them. This is what any college really helps you with. It's a great place to learn from people.

My Take on Academics

I was not a staunch believer of grades and, regretfully, was occasionally not very punctual with my assignments. My pursuits were based on wanting to learn and understand new stuff rather than wanting to work on grades. My grades were fairly decent throughout college, but they were never a priority for me.

One of my regrets is that we could not see to it that the products we built ever reached the market because we were too involved in academics. I think we study too much. In my opinion, in your undergraduate, they should reduce the *compulsion* for students to study and let them pursue what they want to. Academically inclined students would do well regardless, but the onus is more on the student and less on the system. In a sense, more like life and less like school. This is a great time for students to experiment, build projects and really get to understand the product market. It's a very pivotal time where our paradigm transitions from the theoretical to the real-world scenarios and learning more about yourself through new experiences.

Core Projects

My first-year internship was something I tried out with a professor I liked—Professor RKK, one of the founding professors of the computer science department. He was an absolutely brilliant person. He may be a tad bit idiosyncratic, but overall, he was an amazing personality.

For my internship, we built an audio transcoding mechanism for NPTEL so that you can transcribe audio messages directly into captions. It was interesting to work on.

I worked on two projects after that. One was my official BTP (B.Tech Project) in computer vision, and I got my work sponsored by DRDO.

Then, I took up a project with Gaurav Raina. I worked with the Mobile Payments Forum of India on securing the monetary transaction systems that served as a sort of precursor to the UPI services we use today.

I gained a lot of industry experience through these projects. Starting up was still not on my agenda, but I developed a great sense of what it is like to build a product and to make it work the way we intend it to.

Initiation to the world of research

Research still held some importance to me. I had a very fixed notion about what research was. In my head, research was a kind of environment where you were left alone with your devices, and you could do whatever you wanted once you found a problem to work on. But my time at **Microsoft Research during a summer internship** shifted my views dramatically. I realized that research also has its own rat race, much like everything else, and wasn't as collaborative as I would like my work in real life to be. I don't mean that negatively, but it opened my eyes to the reality of how every domain of work has its own carrot and stick—its own progression and hierarchy.

But apart from that realization, I also found that it is really hard to make any relevant impact with your research. It is doable, yes, but a lot of factors come into play. Things like your institute, your professors, the problem space that you choose, and the past progress made in that area. It's found that it is tremendously hard to do impactful research, even in a field that is as young as computer science.

Starting up Vs. Product building

I don't think starting up should be a priority for you in college, especially if you are in an IIT. As students, we should focus more on building products that solve a problem. This product-centered approach is what the current startup culture in India lacks.

We get dragged into putting a different front to ourselves. We put on a blazer and go around claiming, *"I'm in a startup!"* We get sucked into this world of attracting investors and talking to established entrepreneurs and potential VCs. I think that is a terrible way to start a venture.

College is a great time to actually cultivate **product understanding**. Because business skills can be acquired later in your life. But in later life, you will not find yourself in the midst of so many learning opportunities and so much time to spare. Experiment! Explore problems that need to be solved and find a worthy one to work on.

Product-centered thinking is what makes any startup work. Everything else is secondary for technology startups. We need to ask ourselves the right questions to solve the right problems.

Is my product solving a problem for my users?

How can I better my product to meet the needs of users?

When you evaluate your product from a user's perspective, you just know what to do next. That is what will enable you to grow organically and take your product further.

The Tech Angle—the thing about tech startups in India

The people who get deeply excited about the technology behind their products will find the drive to attract grants or sponsorship because what they believe in is the end product, and the investors can see that too. But as someone who is building a product, if you have not built enough empathy about who your users are, you are never going to incite a wave in your field of technology.

User-centered product focus is very important. I think that is what the tech ecosystem in India lacks in comparison to the valley.

Like Snapchat. It would have never come out of India. And what is surprising is that there is no technical reason why Facebook or Snapchat could not have happened in India. We have a larger number of people. We have more college density than foreign universities. The technology was also very simple when it first kicked off. So, all the odds seemed to be in our favor *except* for the reason that culturally, we were too obsessed with fitting into a plan from the outside. We don't have an inside-out plan. We have a very fixed notion of what a business plan looks like. Somewhere, we lose focus on what really matters and get too obsessed with following that plan. We need to learn how to put users above everything else and move our ideas at the speed of our users' wants and needs.

That feeling when people like your product and use your product! We don't have a sense of that feeling. We don't know that joy when somebody takes your product, suddenly finds it organically, starts using it, and it goes crazy. The joy of building something that others like doesn't exist. That is what needs to change.

Placements season

Before you take something up, you need to ask yourself why—at an existential level almost:

> Does it make me more financially secure?
>
> Does it give me a more realized sense of independence?
>
> Or is it a sense of achievement that I am looking for?

You need to realize what sort of incentives drive you. That understanding is important. You have to be comfortable and at peace with the decisions you are making.

In my case, I was very clear that I wanted to do something that I liked doing, with the people who liked doing what they were doing and the challenge ahead of us. If I didn't get to do that, I told my parents that I'd be happy sitting in my parents' basement reading books and watching movies.

So, after my fifth year, I did not sit for placements. I made it very clear to my parents beforehand that I don't care about that at all. Placements would only have served as a distraction, and getting a job was not on my list at the time. They panicked. They talked to my aunts and uncles as parents would. One of my uncles told them to take it easy. He asked them to let me do whatever I wanted. In hindsight, I didn't really present this as a choice to my parents in the first place, and they were kind and trusting enough to relent.

And so, I did that. These first few years were tremendously fun but hard because I was pumping all my earnings from my freelance tech consulting gigs for various companies into running a small team that later came to form our consulting company, **34 Cross**.

Treading the Entrepreneurial path

Soon after graduating, I wanted to get my hands dirty and work on a "real product". I started work on **Brass Plate** with **Rajoshi**. It was a homemade food delivery startup in Chennai. Through the course of trying to get that to work, I realized that this was an operations problem and not really a technical problem. We did not have the appetite for running an *ops-heavy* startup that would be super low-margin.

Owlink was one of the first products we built as an intern training project, which got natural and organic adoption. That feeling was amazing. People picked it up and started using it out of the blue.

Over the course of these projects—products that we built and products that we helped other teams build—we grew our consulting firm to be pretty successful financially, working with financial firms, software companies, and research labs.

All through this time, we had a core set of people working and thinking deeply about developer tools that would enable people to build products faster. We built tools, and then we *dog-fooded* those tools when we worked on our consulting projects.

The big question

Our firm, 34 Cross, started doing really well from thereon. It reached a point where we were reaching 85% of gross margins and bringing in millions of dollars of revenue from our cutting-edge technology work with clients.

We realized that we had hit a checkpoint.

The sort of questions that we had now were very different from the ones we had before.

Do we become the next generation of Infosys?

Or do we just focus on the tools that we built, which have been powering our productivity?

We decided to raise VC and start **Hasura** as a company that would take our technology tooling to developers. Even though I was initially against VC, I realized the reality of there not being enough time to do *everything*. Building and taking a product to market is very different from building a consulting firm.

I was very opinionated. I didn't want to move to the US. I didn't want to raise venture capital. Looking back at this today, we've done all of those things and done a 180-degree turn. But the most important thing is that I had a lot of clarity in the fact that ultimately, solid value needs to be added to people. How you do it is secondary. Everything can change in the service of delivering that value within an ethical framework. This allowed me and the core team to keep moving quickly.

Hasura

The Ethos

We had a couple of things to sort out before we started work on our next venture. When we shut down the consulting firm, we were 50 people. We spent another two quarters getting all of them recruited by other companies and got them working with clients. We helped everybody out. For a lot of them, it was their first job, and being "let go" from your first job is not a fun prospect, to say the least. It was a big deal.

The thing is, you have to do right by people. There is no systemic hack to this. Meet them where they are. Be fair to them. Respect the amount of time they've put in.

For some people, that doesn't matter; they just want a salary. But we care very deeply about our people. If you don't set up false expectations, you won't be disheartened if you have outgrown them or they have outgrown you. You just find a better place in the company for them.

Our core team from **34 Cross**, our consulting firm, came over with us to work at **Hasura**—a VC seed-funded tech startup.

Foundation

Rajoshi Ghosh was my co-founder in Hasura. We had worked together since Brass Plate, Owlink, and all the way through 34 Cross. We had an excellent rapport.

She comes from a computational biology research background. She worked in research for two years and then moved out of research to teaching programming in Ghana for a year at an early-stage tech incubator. Rajoshi and I were introduced because her younger sister was a junior at IIT. From a conversation at the Central Library, she remembered that I was doing some "entrepreneurship" thing and decided to make an introduction!

Two other pivotal people in the Hasura founding team are Anand and Vamshi. **Anand**, a friend from my college days and my "co-core" at Shaastra, went to IIM and then joined Airtel Africa. Vamshi was a CS junior who left his Day Zero placement offer to join Hasura. I knew Vamshi because of a project he'd done with us during our consulting firm days.

We open-sourced our technology work after starting Hasura. Within a year, there was tremendous adoption. Then, that open-source adoption gradually converted into commercial adoption with the commercial offerings that we launched in early 2020. There were no sales; it was just people picking up the product, using it, and coming to us to buy the enterprise version or the cloud version of the product. It was all product-led, just like we'd wanted and hoped for!

People

It's an amazing experience to meet passionate people and get to work with them without having known them before. I remember the very first person who joined us when we were working from our tiny flat in Besant Nagar. He had come in from Delhi. When he reached our "flat" office, he saw that there was no board that indicated that this was a company office. He just saw the three people sitting in front of screens. But he's become a critical part of our journey, and he still works with us! It has been seven years since!

With people, it's all about meeting them where they are and doing right by them, and expecting them to do right by you. It's all about setting up honest expectations. You have to be inspiring and charming, but also very real.

"Listen, this might fail. We will fight like crazy to survive and thrive. I can pay you this salary, and this is your equity in this company we're building together. This is what we will do. And no matter what, you will go with a great learning experience."

In the software industry, professionals are at a much lesser risk because every single place of work provides tremendous learning experiences, whether it's successful or not.

For an early-stage team, I think the binding quality among all of us, the founding team, our early colleagues, is tremendous mental stamina and emotional strength. Those qualities, along with a cultural and ethical alignment, are good prerequisites to work and ride the wave together.

Some Hard Choices

We have also been good at shutting things down. While working on a project, we have realized that this has been a good learning experience, but now, it's time to close it. And some of those decisions have been hard. We went from making zero money to not making money for the first month to having reduced salaries for the next few months to having a lot of money and deciding where to invest it. Those decisions are going to be undoubtedly hard.

But that's what we are good at. Our core team is good at making hard decisions.

"This is not working. We need to change the way we do things. This has to be changed."

And then, we align our people. We ensure that we keep our team's morale up.

For Hasura, we were not planning to make it open-source. We wanted a revenue-based system, and the thing was that it was a good platform, but it wasn't going anywhere as a closed source infrastructure component in the world today. People liked it, but there was no developer-led viral growth. So, we made a tough decision. We removed a lot of extra features for the platform. And we focused on one part, and we open-sourced it. This was not an easy call, but we all deliberated, and it worked out in the end.

I still remember the day. It was an afternoon in San Francisco when we realized we needed a drastic shift in our approach. When we decided to go ahead and move to an open-source model, we made sure we deeply thought about the "why" and how a business model would emerge. We've collected a lot of insight over the last few months, and that's why we decided to go ahead with it! And it picked up. The best decisions made are the ones made together, and then, crazy-fast execution to enjoy the roller-coaster.

Chapter 15

A Ladder to the Moon

Rajiv Srivastava: Co-Founder & COO, Urban Ladder & Antler

Mad(e) for Computers!

My love story with technology began in the 10th grade when I got my first computer and tried my hands on coding. My computer science teacher at school was the wingman in this story. He introduced us to programming in such a phenomenal manner that I couldn't resist falling in love with computers and programming. A passion was instilled in me, and I looked forward to his tests, and every successful attempt at those tests gave me a dopamine rush.

There was not a single subject in my 12 years of education that I was involved in as passionately as in Computer Science. Seeing the code 'Hello World' appear on screen was a magical experience. Using programming to make graphics, computations, and things come to life had a 'kid in a candy shop' feel for me. You could call me a full-blown nerd for all practical purposes!

Naval Architecture Engineering at IITM

My love for computers continued into IIT. I could not get into the CSE branch in an IIT with my rank. But I got into Naval Architecture Engineering instead, a branch which I didn't understand at all. However, given the network and brand effects in the late 1990s, there was no looking back from that decision!

I was always a jack of all trades. I managed to get good grades despite a rocky start. My love for computers never diminished, and I spent a lot of time coding various applications inside Naval Architecture and even went to a programming class on the side. I learned a plethora of programming languages and their application in the real world.

For me, the best part of college was my friends and cricket! I was a day scholar for the most part but was in the hostel in the first year and final year mainly to play cricket for the IITM team. This gave me a balance between experiencing hostel life while also getting a flavor of the outside world.

Programming Projects

I loved all my courses that had *anything* to do with computers. I made an Indian version of Carmen San Diego's game (a game popular in the 1990s). It was a detective game, and I hosted it on our Naval Computer Laboratory server. My juniors and batchmates played it a lot. I felt thrilled to have implemented that project successfully.

My last project was MATLAB (a proprietary multi-paradigm programming language) based. In my last assignment, I simulated ship movements across some water tests. I got a perfect 10 in this project, and it even helped me raise my final grade just above 8. This last project was one of my best works at IIT and gave me the feeling that I was on the right track. I believed that computers were my forte.

Infosys vs. MBA—GDs are not a joke!

While I was considering appearing for the CAT exam, I got into Infosys as a Software Engineer through an on-campus opportunity. As soon as I got that news, nothing else mattered. It was never even a question—a coding job at Infosys (a top company those days on campus) was like a dream come true.

But since I had already paid the exam fees for CAT, I thought, '*Why not give it a shot?*' I did not expect anything from the exam since I was not prepared at all. (In contrast to many of my friends who were really giving it their all in terms of preparation.)

But a somewhat surprising turn of events took place. They changed the pattern of the papers entirely, and those who were accustomed to the previous pattern didn't do well. I just appeared for the exam without much preparation, but I still got calls from five out of the six IIMs at that time.

But I soon realized that IIM was no cakewalk, as things started to get very real in the Group Discussion Round. I was reminded, rather jolted, that I did not have any social skills at the time and could not even articulate myself in English properly. IIM Ahmedabad and IIM Bangalore were very technical, and I was not at all prepared. IIM Calcutta felt like a ragging session to me as I was overwhelmed and clueless!

But two years later, when I took the same exam, I was more prepared, especially for the Group Discussions and interviews. The previous failure is what helped me prepare much better and get into IIM Bangalore.

The Infosys Journey

The first three months in Infosys were very rigorous. You have to learn a bunch of coding languages and also get to work across different teams and compete with some of the brightest minds across the country. My passion for computers really took off at Infosys. I went from being an Okay student to being one of the top 10 people from that batch of 500 at Infosys. It felt very exhilarating. I was doing something I really liked and was also good at it.

The two years (2000–2002) at Infosys really changed me. I worked on a massive side project —a personal website. Over 1000 people each day visited the website, and it was a thrill to see it grow. I incorporated a music player in it (similar to Winamp of olden days) where you could create and edit online playlists and download music.

My first flight ever was to San Francisco, where I implemented a project. Traveling abroad so early on in my career gave me a significant confidence boost. Seeing all these people interact with something that I had created was a feeling beyond anything else. I wanted to chase that feeling everywhere I went.

IIM—Toward Impact & Legacy

After another CAT attempt (this time a successful one), I joined IIM Bangalore for my MBA.

This is where I met Ashish (who later co-founded Urban Ladder with me). Unlike IIT, at IIM, I tried my best to explore everything. I worked on many of the campus clubs and committees: the Placement Team, the Alumni association, the Management Fest committee, the IT club, etc. There was not a single extracurricular activity that I was not a part of.

I also became a lot more social and involved with campus activities than ever before in my life. I decided it was essential to know people. I knew—by name—every single person on campus in my senior batch, my batch, and junior batch. That's over 600 folks across a small span of just two years, and that felt very good. Some of these folks became great friends for life and became the first set of investors, referrers, customers, etc., in every single one of my initiatives later.

Two of the proudest moments at IIMB—which later impacted my entire view on entrepreneurship and building impact: I single-handedly created the intranet 'Spidi' (which lasted more than a decade)—everything from the name, the logo, the product, etc. Along with Spidi, we also launched 'bRacket,' which became the lifeline of the campus communication (these were pre-Facebook/ pre-messenger days).

The other big one for us was our stupendously successful management fest. We got C. K, Prahalad, P. Chidambaram, and Siddhartha Basu for each of the three days of the festival—a coup of sorts for those times. We changed the trajectory of the institution with the fest.

I ended up getting the Gold Medal for Best All-Round Student for the number of activities I either championed or participated in. I really felt like I had blossomed in IIMB. I think the confidence I gained from working at Infosys really boosted my morale to excel across all fronts at IIMB.

Cognizant

I started working at Cognizant later on in 2004 as a Senior Business Analyst. Cognizant was a coveted technology job from campus (there were no product jobs during the 2004 season). I had the opportunity to come back to Chennai and also work in a great team.

It was a fascinating work atmosphere, and I felt like I fit right in. With accelerated learning and fast career growth at Cognizant, I got the opportunity to go to Switzerland in 2007. However, I realized this was a totally different ball game. Selling enterprise services was a totally different experience, and my heart was beating for the Internet.

I loved the business analysis work at Cognizant but not the sales part. Plus, Switzerland was boring to live in. I lacked the network that I had in India, and it felt pretty bland to me. Today, it would be very different, but I had a very rigid mindset back then.

Yahoo! And the Internet

I thought of shifting to internet companies now, and I applied to a bunch of them, including Google Switzerland and every internet company in India. I landed a job at Yahoo! India. My wife and I resigned and came back to India (and Bangalore). I became a Product Manager with Yahoo!

Four years at Yahoo! were pretty fantastic. I learned what internet products were and how to work with them. Products like Yahoo! Finance, Yahoo! Cricket (First ICC partnership), Yahoo! Movies, Yahoo! News, etc. These first products changed the trajectory of Yahoo! India to become one of the most important media destinations for Yahoo! across the world. Many of these properties became #1 in their categories. This also gave me great exposure to working across different teams such as content, marketing, advertising, business development, etc., in addition to working with very strong engineering products and UX teams.

The best experience at Yahoo! happened toward the second half of my career there. I launched Yahoo! India Education from scratch. The entire customer research process, building from nothing, reaching millions of users, and building this product like a small startup within Yahoo! gave me a ton of confidence. We also launched Yahoo! Stars, a celebrity-focused social product that was an iPad's first experience. Once again, despite not fully taking off, it gave me the first true sense of intrapreneurship in the internet world.

As it so often happens in many corporations, after four years at Yahoo!, I was making more presentations justifying building products than actually building products. This was the time I decided to start off on my own.

The Ascent into entrepreneurship

I started talking with Ashish Goel (wing mate from IIMB). We used to catch up during dinner. In September 2011, we were driving in Indiranagar and decided let's do an online grocery shopping site. For the next two to three months, we met with many investors.

We talked to Kanwal from Helion (the first VC in my life). Venture capitalists were new at that time and rather limited.

While all these discussions were in progress, we started using our connections to understand the grocery market better. The market was undoubtedly big, but we wanted to be more than just the traders. We wanted to build on something more product-based.

After dozens of ideas in education, media, etc., we realized lifestyle E-commerce is where it was getting big. We first thought of doing a portal for women, but Vani Kola (Kalaari Capital, who later became our first investor at Urban Ladder) said there are already big players in that area, like Myntra and Jabong. We would be better off going after a less penetrated category. We chose home decor and furniture as that focused on the category we wanted to win.

Urban Ladder—The First months

By December 2011, we decided to go with furniture and named it Urban Ladder.

We first thought of sourcing from Bangalore, but Vani suggested we try out Jodhpur. For the next few months, we started working on setting the company up. Before we launched, Kalaari Capital (VC) gave us a term sheet in April, and we raised our $1 Mn.

We got our first employee, first office space, and first funding in the first part of 2012. The initial idea mainly was that we'll work as a technology provider and provide an amazing buying experience to the customers from different spaces. For initial customers, we started sharing our products on Facebook.

Our friends and college ecosystem from IIT and IIM started helping in spreading the word. The image of being the 'trustworthy' people helped. Reliability is an asset you will always need while building a business. And it is something that you have to develop consistently.

Our friends started buying and posting on social media. We started using Facebook very well because, at that time, feeds weren't paid. That combined with word of mouth, we reached from 0 to 1 crore in a month, and our burn rate was mainly office employees and rent. Therefore, we were operationally profitable.

The Consumer Experience

We had limited categories; pretty much everything was hand-chosen. We were delivering only in Bangalore, Delhi, and Mumbai, with our Vision of 'Making millions of homes Beautiful'.

We allowed people to give honest reviews. Instead of deleting bad ones, we replied and worked our best on fixing them. We were scaling slowly but with a lot more focus on excellence. In two years, we were in three cities at a revenue of 2 crores/month with a burn rate of Rs. 20-25 lakhs/month. We had raised $6Mn in two years. Thankfully, Kalaari, SAIF Partners, and our other investors were long-term thinkers and were not pushing us for unsustainable growth.

The crazy scale-up years

Then, in the next two years (2015, 2016), we raised $70 million! We grew *exponentially*. But we also committed a lot of scale mistakes that used up capital much faster than we anticipated.

As soon as you start raising a lot of funds, you start getting bigger challenges to handle. We had raised $7 million in two and a half years. But the moment we raised $70 million, all things went south. If you raised so much cash, you're expected to grow at 4X every year. We started sourcing from China, expanded our catalog five times its size, got into a fancy office, and hired four times our team size in one year.

When you start doing so many extra things, the revenue growth has to keep up with the burn rate. 2015 was the year where we grew rapidly, and as a side effect, we became very undisciplined and reckless. Our revenues grew 12 times, but our burn rate rose by 75 times— which, in hindsight, is quite silly. But we thought we would deliver as we were investing more resources.

This, compared to the 2012 to 2014 period, was the opposite side of the coin. As we expanded our catalog, we could not keep up with the quality and design. It turned out to be very detrimental in terms of scaling.

There was phenomenal growth between 2015-16, but that growth blinded us to a lot of our mistakes. We realized that it was not a very sustainable growth model as it was fueled by venture capital.

Damage Control

We started pulling back in April of 2016. But there are some things which you can pull back fast, and there are others which you can't. We pulled back TV advertising and marketing activities. But the products which got piled up took nearly six to nine months to get cleared. We moved from a fancy office in September 2016 to a more reasonable office by Sep 2017. A lot of things took time.

We realized that we had to be more frugal. We also have the strategy of going omnichannel in retail because in the case of online, for every extra rupee of revenue, we have to spend two rupees in marketing. Therefore, we decided to give offline stores a shot. It obviously took a lot more time. It took some 8 to 12 months to develop on its own, from designing as a store to bringing furniture, etc. Thankfully, by doing all these pull-back initiatives, we reduced the burn by 80% and increased revenue by 20%. The Sep 2016—Apr 2018 period was one of the best turnarounds for learning and development.

CEO Versus Entrepreneur

As an entrepreneur, you have accelerated learning. You get the learning you would have got in 15 years in a job in 5 years. The high points are very exhilarating, but the lows take a lot of your energy away too.

You can get really mentally impacted by all of these events—people not joining your firm, having to do layoffs, a bad investor presentation, lower than expected revenues, friction with co-founders or founding teams, negative press, key initiatives not taking off, a competitor getting far higher funding despite bad customer reviews, etc.

That's the difference between wearing a co-founder hat and the CEO hat. When you are a small firm, as co-founders, you are at the same level, and you sort of divide responsibilities, but the moment the team becomes 200 to 300 people, you need to have a very clear and precise segregation of duties. There is a lot of maturity which needs to be ingrained as a co-founder— something we took too long to realize.

We did not have the guidance that we required to foresee the consequences of our mistakes. There were not as many entrepreneurial guides or advisors then as there are today. We had to hit the ground running for every issue that we were facing and then try to solve it the best way possible.

The departure

After 2018, we decided to go for external fundraising. I decided that after this fundraise, I'd move out because Urban Ladder became more of an omnichannel furniture single brand retailer while I wanted to be more into the technical side. After doing this for seven years, I realized there are people much better than me in building the omnichannel business. I also felt it was time for me to go and do something else.

Unfortunately, the external fundraising took longer than expected and, ultimately, did not happen. By March 2019, we were not able to get funding. We had to shed some of the business, and along with that, unfortunately, we had let go of ~30% of people because we were not able to raise external money.

By enacting all these measures, we got into the zero-burn territory, albeit on a lesser revenue scale. This happened by July 2019, around our seventh anniversary. Although this was not the way I would have wanted to move out, I still decided to move on and do something else since you cannot hang around in limbo as a founder. You are either firing on all cylinders, or you should make your way out. I had overstayed my tenure by more than a year, waiting for the right outcome, which never came. Although I obviously felt bad that this was not the ending I had hoped for, it was time for the next move.

Post facto, Urban Ladder was acquired in November 2020 by Reliance. Because of COVID, we were highly impacted, and the capital situation had become dire. So, Reliance brought a very different and new life to Urban Ladder and started a new journey. Enough has been written in the press as a post-mortem after that deal, but it was a surreal experience to see this entire journey right from the center for 7 years and then from the sidelines for the last 1.5 years.

Antler—Falling in love with new beginnings for the new decade

At Urban Ladder, the journey was amazing. It didn't teach me just about business, but it also made me realize my passion areas that I could shine at and be in full flow.

I realized that I enjoyed the initial parts of building a startup a lot more than the later stages when things were more process-oriented. That's what led me to start Antler in India. I want to help champion and inspire thousands of potential entrepreneurs and prepare them for the 10+ years of ups and downs of the founder journey. Because this journey is like a sine wave. It's filled with massive positive and negative swings. While I love building, I would also want to be a coach and facilitator to many others during my Antler journey.

I consider building Antler itself like building a startup. We are building a tech-enabled institution that is going to create thousands of tech-enabled solutions. It's like building a startup that is helping build thousands of startups. For me, this is a massive mandate and also a global one at that. Being in the business of ideas helps challenge me across many spaces. This is also about building a brand, getting together hundreds of smart minds in the form of a team and thousands of founders, and building a tech product that helps all of this globally. I am as excited about this journey as I was when I sat for the first time at a computer 25 years back!

One Life Theory—And spreading happiness to millions

The other topic that I was personally excited about in the last five years of my life—between 2016 and 2021—is the field of happiness. Just around the start of Covid and before taking on the Antler mandate, I also started a podcast around spreading happiness and human potential. In this decade, this is the other big charter that I have taken up—spreading personal impact and potential to tens of millions of people globally.

A lot of people, especially early in their adult life and in their mid-life, are stuck in a middling zone without knowing what to do in their lives. The purpose of OneLifeTheory is to make millions live their life to their fullest. I hope to achieve this through content, counseling sessions, and a community that can support each other through their life journeys. The idea is to be a jack of all trades all over again—very similar to the way I have lived life through my prime years across the last 20 years.

Chapter 16

Faster than the Speed of Light

Kedar Kulkarni: Hyperverge

Kedar embodies the technological fire that stokes at the heart of an IITian. From his first year, he was devoted to pursuing knowledge and technological disruption. With Kedar, it was never about how many times you fell down. It's about how many times you get back up and continue to push on.

With his first educational startup, Lema Labs, he and his team successfully proved that age is no bar for making a difference in the world. Hyperverge started as a Computer Vision Research Group in the Centre for Innovation, IIT Madras. They developed technological solutions for Indian Railways, ITC, MRF, etc.

Fasten your seatbelts while you witness this fantastic journey of young minds with a mission.

The IITM Culture

After the grueling JEE preparations, I wanted a taste of campus culture and to be able to finally spread my wings. When I came to the IITM campus, I wanted to do everything I could. I participated in sports and got involved in technical clubs. I even tested the waters of literature while scriptwriting for college short films. Standing for elections and volunteering in Shaastra were also my college experience highlights.

Through my avid participation in various events, I got the chance to interact with many people. I came to find my tribe with the Tech crowd from CFI (Centre for Innovation). They were highly mission-driven and cared about finishing what they started. My affinity for the technological field increased exponentially through my interaction with the group.

IARC

I found out that IITM was putting together a team to enter the **International Aerial Robotics Competition (IARC)**, one of the most challenging aerial robotics competitions globally. This competition was known to have very tough problem statements. Even the best colleges in the world, like MIT and Georgia Tech, which are known for their advancements in Robotics, took four to five years to develop a solution.

Ravi Kant, the then head of CFI, had the audacity to say that we could do this. Being a part of this team exposed me to the vast universe of Electronic Tech. The number of challenges was commensurate with the scale of the project. We worked on it for a year but did not participate because our progress was not up to the mark. Going to the **International Conference on Robotic Computing (IRC)** meant that we had to put together a budget of 20 lakhs, and we wouldn't get to do it more than once a year. So, even if the institute was sponsoring us, we had to make sure that it was worth the costs. The robot itself cost us seven lakhs. Next year, I was supposed to lead the computer vision team.

The problem statement read along these lines... There has been a nuclear meltdown. Your quadcopter has to fly about two kilometers to enter that zone. Once it enters the zone, it has to find its way directly to the target building without detours. Then, the device has to take pictures of the site and come back to the starting location.

In this crazy problem statement, computer vision played an important role. We were clueless about how to incorporate this in our first year. While forming our team next year, we took in about 20 promising candidates and decided to train them. There were some dropouts by the end of it. But those who ended up staying worked very hard. Our last three months were full of breakthroughs, and our robot was working fantastically at the end of them. We were finally ready to participate.

IITM Computer Vision Group (CVG)

We didn't win the prize, but our robot had the best computer vision system among the participating projects. We realized that we could beat even some world-class institutes if we took a problem-centered approach. After coming back, we started a group called the Computer Vision Group, which exists in IITM even today. The following year we took around 50 students to train, and a few of them stuck with us. All the co-founders of Hyperverge came through this program of ours.

After a year, we discussed what the future of CVG would be and deliberated on two things that we wanted to achieve. If we solve a real problem for a firm, they should either

1. be ready to pay for it, or

2. conduct our research on that problem and go for a patent.

Henceforth, whatever projects we took on should lie in these two categories. This understanding sowed its seeds for me in the first year itself. The other clubs' projects were fascinating, but they did not sum up to anything concrete in the long run. I realized that this was merely a hobby for many people—something to pass the time in college and get to put on your CV.

Even the technically proficient senior was doing a banking job.

There was a broad idea among juniors that what we were doing was just for fun and could not go beyond aesthetics.

We realized that we could not progress anywhere as a group unless we converted this into something that started paying money and solving real problems.

Lema Labs

Lema Labs was an educational startup that I co-founded in my third year. It got our wheels rolling. We broke the illusion that we, as college students, could not go out there and solve real-world problems.

Hero Handa

During campus placements, I came across Mr. Sunil Handa. He is an entrepreneur who has created more than 500 entrepreneurs. He's also a professor at IIM Ahmedabad. I attended one of his lectures at our campus, and it changed everything I thought I knew about entrepreneurship.

In his lecture, Handa Sir told us about his life. He thought his potential was wasted sitting at a desk doing a job. And so, he quit, and he and his brother toyed with various entrepreneurship ideas, some of which even failed. After experimenting with eight ideas, they finally "struck gold" with their ninth one. His Core Emballage, a pharmaceutical manufacturing company, became India's largest manufacturer of IV fluids in the second year of its operation and later became the third-largest in the world. The net worth of the company was over $240 million by 1998. Clearly, it shows that persistence is the key. The opportunities lie scattered around the world; we just need to dig them out for ourselves.

I learned that entrepreneurship was not about ideas but a lifestyle. Hyperverge was not even created by that time. We were all still part of CVG and were working on projects. We were not making a lot of money out of them. But Lema Labs was bringing in some revenue. The question arose, "How do we sustain to continue doing what we're doing?"

After college, I decided not to go for a job but to work full-time as the CEO of Lema Labs. The good thing about this was that I used to have a lot of free time. Throughout the day, I was working on Lema Labs, more on the business side of things, and by evening I was back at the CVG base. We had a couple of projects going on at the time. We deliberated that we would not be lazy and fritter our time away—credits to Handa Sir for unlocking this energy and motivating us to keep at it.

Parents kya kahenge? (What on earth will parents say?)

At that time, startups had not gained as much momentum as now.

I took my parents to meet many professors and the Dean, and each had a very significant contribution because every one of them told them just to let this guy do whatever he wants to do. "In some years, you will see the results. Don't worry about it."

Hearing this was some comfort to my parents. They figured out that the professors knew what they were saying. If they believe this is the right path for him, let him continue.

Intermediate Projects

One day Krishna Pal Subramanyam Sir, Dean of ICSR, came for one of the CFI exhibitions and saw our technology. We managed to impress him. Mahesh Sir, the then Dean, was a mechanical professor at the time and was very enthusiastic. He had a look at what we were doing and supported us for it. Some of the other professors, too, began looking at our work and gave their inputs. When Southern Railway reached out to Professor Krishna, he gave us the problem statement. He even helped us make the draft after we solved the problem at hand.

Hyperverge

The Problem statement provided by the Professor was very big and had immense revenue potential. Even if they gave us an order of 10 systems, it would produce ten crores in revenue.

We did a lot of work to show the client how we arrived at a solution. We presented our work to the Railway board. But we could not land the contract though we ended up registering Hyperverge. We were sitting in my apartment, thinking of naming our group. KV (Vignesh Krishnakumar) came through with the name Hyperverge, which meant beyond limits. We were very frustrated with the Indian Industry after that point. We decided to take Hyperverge to the USA and start from scratch.

The TECHtonic Shift

So far, we had been working on traditional machine learning techniques. But in 2013, we realized that we had never explored the domain of deep learning. Using deep learning concepts, we were able to get 90% accuracy as compared to the 50% we used to get initially. We knew that this technology would be very powerful, given a few years. It was not up to par with the industry expectation back then.

We invested in two major technologies, scene and face recognition. We decided to build an app that works similar to what Google photos are today.

We laid down $80,000 on the further development of the application on a small Kickstarter campaign. But we knew that the technology we were working on was far more potent than the app itself. Deep learning made it possible to go beyond 95% accuracy, which is pivotal for critical functions in day-to-day life. This was the future of AI.

The perfect storm

The combination of AI and Cloud capacities made it possible to develop solutions that would perform at a thousandfold the speed of humans and be almost as accurate. We decided to build an app that combines these capacities.

Raising Funds

So, KV and I went to New York to test the markets and set up in the US. We met a senior named Shara at our first meeting in New York. He said, "You guys are onto something. You should raise more money."

When we inquired how much, he answered, "$300,000."

Our expenditure for the last two years didn't add up to $10,000. How would we go about raising $300,000?

He said, "If you don't, Google or Facebook will be working on this technology."

We were meeting advisors in the Bay Area. Every weekend, we would go to whoever called us. We would pitch our ideas for $10–$20,000 in funding but to no avail. Each night, we would come back and analyze what went wrong and what worked in our favor. We had very little money to go on at the time and couldn't even afford a hotel. We would simply save every rupee that we could. Somehow, we had decided that we would not come back from the US unless funded. After meeting some of our advisors, we realized that the problem was with our pitch. Based on the questions that we often got asked, we revamped our entire pitch to answer all those questions. After that, we started getting very different responses from the investors. We went from the point where we were struggling to get angel investors on board to the point where we began piquing the interest of VC firms.

212 | The IITM Nexus

We ended up registering our company in the US and figured out all the things to do. We thought about approaching NEA (New Enterprise Associates) for funding. Someone told us that NEA does not fund anything under one to $2 million. We ended up meeting Kittu to seek his advice. We found that he was very supportive of us but told us that we should have approached him earlier. In two days, we had three meetings at NEA. They said that they were ready to invest half a million dollars at $4 million valuations within a week. By that time, we already had three VCs on board. That is where our narrative began to change as a company.

Google steals the show

We built and launched an app that was called Silver. It could be used to sort your photos and search for people and particular places. We were into our first month when Google launched Google Photos. It made automated storage accessible, was going to be the default app on every android phone, and had the search capability that we were offering.

Our VCs were already skeptical about us trying our consumer products because they thought it was safer to work with enterprises. But we were adamant that we wanted to work with consumers. After Google came into the picture, a lot of them started to tell us, "I told you so."

We then built an app called Magic shell. But that did not catch a lot of consumer base either. We had money to go to next year's May or June; we were out of all ideas. One thing that hit us hard was that while consumer apps felt like we would be masters of our feed, we realized that building a consumer app is just a small technological problem. To gain success, we needed to onboard the majority of the student population. For a few years, our team of some most competent people worked on figuring out ways to woo our users. This period made me question the whole purpose of what we were doing.

Why were we wasting man-hours on something that our consumers will waste their time on?

Is social media a worthwhile endeavor for us to pursue?

Million Dollar Ballpark figures

This was also the time when AI was very hot. People started acquiring companies left, right, and center at that time. Amazon, Alibaba, Microsoft, etc., everyone was acquiring companies. Most of them were getting good exits. We started getting emails from Microsoft, Alibaba, and other tech companies.

We got a mail from Amazon. We spoke to Venky, Anand, and some of our other investors. They saw that we had filed for patents.

We built out an extraordinary amount of technology—automatic categorization of photos using face recognition that works even on 2G networks, zero cost and seamless offline photo sharing between multiple devices, AI-based summarization of large albums into 30 best photos, etc. We knew that it would be a minimum of $15 to $20 million acquisition, and we were only a 13-member team back then. At that point, it would mean that every founder makes a few million dollars. Everyone else makes at least a quarter-million dollars. Investors make at least three to four times return on their investment. The investors assured us that this was not the world's end and they would still fund our next company. They urged us to consider an exit.

One part of me was considering an exit because we were running out of time and ideas; the other part said that this could not be the end of our story.

Making Money Vs. Making a difference

Our team of 13 people took some time out to discuss prospects. Many of us came up with alternatives like doing something fundamental in improving healthcare or improving education and improving our country or rural employment. We figured that if making money was our objective, we could just go for the exit, and all of us would be on our way. Some of us could start another company together. If you are looking to work together on a fundamental problem, it makes sense to work together for many years. If it's about money, this exit was as good as what we would get tomorrow. But if we wanted to do something beyond just making money, we had to reconsider our strategies. While the idea was very romantic, we had no way to make it happen. It took a month and a half of searching.

Venky and Anand, our investors/mentors, told us to go and pour our hearts out and not to worry. They would not judge us as investors but rather guide us with their advice every step of the way. Venky mentioned that the idea is great. If you really need to contribute in a big way, you need to stand the test of time. For that, you need to make money while you can.

What does Hyperverge bring to the table?

Sometime in February, we ended up speaking to Sridhar Vembu of Zoho. We learned how to build a large organization that contributes to society and stands the test of time.

The conversation with Vembu was a very honest one. We told him we needed to make money and we did not know how. His reply was simple:

"You need to make half a million dollars this year and some part of it can come from Zoho. Relentlessly focus on surviving on your revenues."

The team worked hard to produce AI engines, most of which hold among the top five accuracies in the world. Sridhar kept his promise and happily so, Zoho became our first paying customer. Our group's average age was 24 years, and it shocked us that someone was ready to pay us a quarter of a million dollars. The difference between 95% to 98% is enormous. It is a technology worth every penny invested. Today, many top brands such as DNV GL, TCS COIN, Digital Globe, FE Credit, Bajaj, and more are partners and paying customers.

The Social Side

We faced two crucial questions which would decide our stance on what we wanted our company to look like:

1. Can we make a large organization contribute to people's lives?

2. Can we build hundreds of leaders who see how such an organization is built?

In the Apr-Jun quarter of 2017, we became cash-flow positive. Following our learning from Zoho University, the first investment we made with our surplus income was buying GPU (Graphics processing unit) infrastructure that we plan to make available to college students who want to learn deep learning.

Another initiative we have is powering nano entrepreneurs by providing a minimal interest 10,000 rupees loan. We also decided to open out our AI Engines to enterprises. Revenue now had a clear purpose. These enterprises would be funded by our revenues and powered by our technological solutions.

We hope to carry on this legacy and establish ourselves as a force to be reckoned with in the startup ecosystem.

The End

It's promising to see that you've stuck with us till the end. This book is the fruit of the patience and efforts of numerous people. As a society, we pass on our learnings so that the next generation does not need to reinvent the wheel and can keep building on past successes.

IIT Madras, as of 2021, has completed 62 years with more than 50,000 alumni which opens up a whole world of possibilities. Our closely-knit Nexus spans all the way from seniors giving their *fundas* to juniors to alumni across the globe who enrich the IIT Madras community by sharing their knowledge and experience.

Entrepreneurs play a significant role in each of our lives. A few of them come to the limelight, but many more operate from behind the curtains.

We hope it was an enjoyable read. Feel free to share your thoughts with us. We would highly appreciate it.

– **Shree and Shibani**

Made in the USA
Monee, IL
07 February 2022